The Notebooks of Sonny Rollins

Edited by Sam V. H. Reese

nyrb **New York Review Books** New York

This is a New York Review Book

published by The New York Review of Books

207 East 32nd Street, New York, NY 10016

www.nyrb.com

Library of Congress Cataloging-in-Publication Data
Names: Rollins, Sonny, author. | Reese, Sam V. H., writer of introduction, editor.
Title: The notebooks of Sonny Rollins / by Sonny Rollins; introduction by Sam
    V. H. Reese ; edited by Sam V. H. Reese.
Description: New York City: New York Review Books, 2024.
Identifiers: LCCN 2023029935 (print) | LCCN 2023029936 (ebook) | ISBN
    9781681378268 (paperback) | ISBN 9781681378275 (ebook)
Subjects: LCSH: Rollins, Sonny—Notebooks, sketchbooks, etc. | Rollins,
    Sonny—Diaries. | Saxophonists—Notebooks, sketchbooks, etc. | Jazz
    musicians—Notebooks, sketchbooks, etc. | Saxophonists—Diaries. | Jazz
    musicians—Diaries.
Classification: LCC ML419.R64 A3 2024 (print) | LCC ML419.R64 (ebook) |
    DDC 788.7/165092—dc23/eng/20230706
LC record available at https://lccn.loc.gov/2023029935
LC ebook record available at https://lccn.loc.gov/2023029936

ISBN 978-1-68137-826-8
Available as an electronic book; ISBN 978-1-68137-827-5

Printed in the United States of America on acid-free paper.

10 9 8 7 6 5 4 3 2

Contents

Introduction

I

IN 1959, SONNY ROLLINS disappeared. At twenty-eight, he was one of the undisputed masters of the saxophone—a former teen prodigy whose early work with Bud Powell, Charlie Parker, and a young Miles Davis had incubated a complex, rhythmically guided mode of composition and improvisation. Rollins's 1957 album *Saxophone Colossus* had cemented both his popularity and his critical standing. In 1958, the leading jazz critic of the era, Gunther Schuller, could confidently describe Rollins as the "central figure" of contemporary jazz improvisation. But after a successful tour of Europe in the first half of 1959, Rollins stopped recording and performing. He would not reappear as an artist until late in 1961.

During the last months of his break from performing, Rollins was discovered in the throes of practicing by the jazz journalist Ralph Berton. Though Berton disguised both Rollins and his whereabouts in the article he wrote about the encounter, the truth quickly got around. For nearly two years, Rollins had been practicing, mostly alone, on the Williamsburg Bridge, sometimes for fifteen-hour stretches. Although he only practiced through the night a handful of times, a particular image took hold: the saxophonist silhouetted against the lights of the New York skyline. It seemed to embody the ideals of jazz—its nocturnal urban spirit, its association with the solitary genius, and its potential for a romantic flow of spontaneous and unpremeditated art. It is hardly surprising that it remains one of the most enduring and repeated visual signifiers of jazz.

The dramatic staging of his practice sessions on the bridge added to Rollins's mystique and gave his next album its title and thematic focus. But his motivation for withdrawing is more revealing. Rollins has since spoken several times about an intense dissatisfaction with his own abilities and achievements that came to a head in 1959. To an observer, these claims might seem baffling. Rollins was ten years into his career. He had performed and recorded with some of the leading figures in bebop. He had recorded more than a dozen albums as a band leader and, since 1955, had been laying down a huge number of pieces that would become jazz standards, including "Oleo," "Doxy," "Airegin," and the calypso-inspired piece that quickly became his trademark, "St. Thomas." But Rollins's virtuosic improvisations were driven by a keen intelligence and intense self-reflection. These qualities were expressed in his playful and frequently underrated 1957 album, *Way Out West*, where Rollins reimagined the cliched soundscape of Western films into an experimental and often beautiful record, and in *Freedom Suite*, a 1958 protest album whose political message so confounded his record company that they decided to retitle, republicize, and rearrange the recording.

The same qualities that propelled his composition and improvisation were also manifested in the way that Rollins approached his period of reflection. In one of his first accounts of those years of withdrawal, an interview in *DownBeat* in late 1961, Rollins explained: "When I quit, I suppose I had the intention of changing myself drastically, my whole approach to the horn." When he "realized after awhile that that wasn't what was needed or what was bothering me," Rollins changed tack and "began to study what I had been doing . . . explored all the possibilities." For two years he followed a disciplined practice schedule, setting himself specific goals that he reevaluated frequently. Musical practice was complemented by physical exercise and meditation. He adopted a strict regimen of reading and research, which blended diverse musicological texts with philosophical and political treatises. And he began to write, usually on a yellow legal pad, but sometimes on pamphlets, photocopies, booklets—whatever happened to be at hand.

The results were a compelling mixture of practical, theoretical, and political observations. Already legendary for the vast range of musical references he could draw on when improvising, Rollins's "study" comprised an idiosyncratic reading list. Classical European composition and musical theory was complemented by notes on the structure of ragas and principles of Hindu music—the start of an enduring engagement with Indian culture and beliefs. But study for Rollins was always two parts practical experimentation for every one part theory. His detailed notes on the placement of one's fingers on the keys and the position of the tongue inside the mouth when playing were frequently accompanied by ink sketches and diagrams. Even for a nonmusician, the startling directness and verve of his style communicates his rethinking of musical concepts in a vivid, tangible way; we feel the tension and excitement when he finishes some observations on whether "a note can be different and yet the same" with the enjoinder "now to see if this implies and bears out what I think . . ."

Rollins's first run of notebooks is riddled with similar instructions. They demonstrate an ethos of resilience, designed to build a "greater awareness" that any difficulties "will be 'conquered' . . .

through time and understanding gradually." Reflections on his progress are intermingled with definitions of relevant words, which Rollins often gives a revealing rewording. "Impulse," for example, is followed by "Obeying an impulse," and then "Relaying the sound of the inner voice"—a definition that precisely captures his determination to connect mind, body, and soul. The apparently haphazard movement across subject matter in the notebooks of this period—jumping from biology to theory to philosophy—is the product not of a disorganized mind but of a syncretic approach to self-reflection and self-development. It is also an expression, in slow motion, of Rollins's ideal of jazz performance, which takes shape over these years: "The instantaneous creation of music—an unbroken link from thought to thing—immediately—at once—intelligently—but with emotion." This note might just as well apply to Rollins's writing; many of his notes trace the same arc from thought to thing, or just as often, thing to thought.

The habit Rollins began during his bridge years would sometimes lapse in future decades. But the notebooks continued to offer a reflective space, to which he would return again and again; when he donated his archive to the New York Public Library in 2017, his personal notebooks took up a hefty six boxes.

2

Rollins left the scene during a year in jazz that, even at the time, was seen as one of momentous transition. The hard-bop style that Rollins had helped to define was branching outwards in one direction into the modal jazz of Davis's *Kind of Blue*, in another towards the free jazz of Ornette Coleman's *The Shape of Jazz to Come*. Stoked by these developments, by stories of Rollins's unique method of woodshedding, and by a few tantalizing interviews, the critical expectations around his next album, *The Bridge* (released in March 1962), reached a feverish pitch. The album found a wide and appreciative audience, and yet critical approval was shadowed with disappointment. Rollins's sound and style had not undergone a complete revolution in the way his peers' had in his absence nor, for all its soul, did his music seem to embrace the overt spirituality cultivated by John Coltrane.

But if they had listened closely to what Rollins had been saying about his withdrawal, critics would have known what to expect. In an interview with the *New Yorker*'s longtime jazz critic Whitney Balliett, in November 1961, Rollins had put his finger on why he'd felt dissatisfied with jazz in 1959. It was not just a question of his own performance. He felt a general dissatisfaction with the world of jazz. "People are not doing things as well as they can do them any more," Rollins said. His goal was not revolution but what he called "mastership," to be achieved incrementally through critical self-evaluation. He titled one section of notes "Against I," and many of his assessments of how well he has followed his own regimen offer a harsh verdict: "Birthday now past but tendencies toward disruption still exist. So I have not fought my desire to violate dietary Truths." Rollins's emphasis on mastery, not change, points to a fundamental realization that would drive his music for the next stage of his career: Jazz had now reached a point where the musical and technical innovations that had propelled it from the outset could no longer be sustained as such. Jazz had to be reconsidered, with a broader historical perspective and more specific individual emphasis.

What Rollins meant by mastery, he told Balliett, was "doing things well."

Often, this challenge seemed frightening enough on its own. In one note he begs himself to "face the startling and intriguing reality that there is within me a force working hard for my own destruction, even as I try to improve." These critiques of his own efforts are not designed to dissuade himself from study and practice. They invoke, instead, a kind of humility, allowing him to shift his focus back towards persistence and resilience. One mantra reads: "Persevere I shall." Other entries offer greater detail on how he figures perseverance: "by the very documenting of these transgressions I am demonstrating my awakening strength which will come into full bloom at such time as I have suffered through the various manifestations of these problems."

Throughout, Rollins continually reevaluates his motivations, reminding himself that "the motive for doing a thing is inevitably and ultimately ABOVE that thing." His list of "Motives and Aims" includes the wish to "uplift and inspire people," and his notebooks repeatedly reflect a belief that jazz could accomplish social good in the world. For Rollins, jazz was "vigorously hybrid," and it was the music's ability to break down artificial racial barriers that saw him align jazz with "the realization of the next American Dream." This realization, towards which his music and his notebooks are both equally directed, is driven by the peculiar energy of jazz as "a derivative music"—derivative not in the sense of being secondhand or worn out but, in Rollins's words, "comprising many elements, peoples, and countries."

While Rollins never sought to downplay the central role that black musicians have played in the history of jazz, the tenor of his social reflections is "equality"—a term that he defines as "The right to be able to do what you ought." He declares in one note that he wants to "destroy the myths which separate not only jazz men of different ethnic backgrounds but indeed all men are plagued by this mistrust and misunderstanding based on fear and ignorance." Rollins had worked with a diverse range of musicians before this point, but when this statement was written, he was collaborating closely with the white guitarist Jim Hall (who features on *The Bridge*). In other notes, Rollins would reflect that "Jim is the class of his instrument. His playing never fails to inspire me." His notes connect equality to sex as well as race, advocating for "equal opportunity to realize individual potential" regardless of "biology." This "regardless" is telling. Rollins's conceptualization of equality is not a question of equal categories but of doing away with categories altogether, and these early notebooks establish an ongoing fear that the very label of jazz could limit or constrain musical expression. For Rollins, racial chauvinism was anathema to the history of musical cross-pollination, where "the Musings of Miles is then the Bouncing of Bach both played against each other."

As he began to return to performing, Rollins also began to consider codifying some of his observations into a book for saxophonists. Now that he had "credentials gleaned from the breast of experience," Rollins felt a new "desire to disseminate proven principles as pertaining to the saxophone and those aspects of music which are indigenous to its mastery." The material he drew up varied as vigorously as his conceptualization of jazz, but one way of tracking his preoccupations is by way of prospective titles—Rollins would regularly jot down new possibilities, often accompanying them with doodles, diagrams, and mock-ups. All love letters to the saxophone, his first set of titles clearly reflects his return to a public stage, to working with peers, and his commitment to leadership: he considered "The Fraternity of Saxophone" and "The Saxophone Brotherhood," along with several variations on these key words. While his notes towards a book do offer some practical advice for navigating the world of performance—"touch[ing] upon those problems of being a professional which will come up during such situations as being on the road"—by far the most common title is "Fantastic Saxophone." In his notebooks, the instrument, often sketched surrounded by radiating light, takes on a mystical, talismanic quality. In the saxophone, he writes, "we saw a better and more beautiful world. We saw, and see the means towards a better human being; towards the perfection of our selves."

These notes for a book also reveal a sensitivity to the stylistic demands of a wider audience. There is a clearer control of narrative, and his tendency towards aphoristic briefness in his personal meditations expands in a more expository, pedagogical manner. In some mock lessons, Rollins even experiments with a colloquial, sometimes sardonic voice—"if it takes a week before you are sure of hitting the next note correctly, wait the week. So who's in a hurry—especially to make a Boo-Boo???!!!"—but mostly he maintains the same well-balanced composition that distinguishes his early notebooks. Balanced phrases like "discovered and learned to appreciate" lend his sentences an elegant rhythm, while his flair for verbal elaboration only increases their charm. Practical inquiries into specific saxophone technique at times branch into questions about the very act of learning. These grow out of earlier, personal notes on his difficulty in replicating particular sounds and effects without embedding them sufficiently in the musical line, but also come from a conceptual interest in the mutable intensity of the experience of time. Rollins now wanted to take the time to cement and iron out each new technique until it was integrated into an individual playing style. He espoused what he called the "Sonny Rollins Pay as You Go Method," which consisted of "stopping when you are ahead and afterwards successfully executing any given passage."

And yet Rollins never completed his book; in the end he felt his approach was too idiosyncratic, too specific to himself to be "applicable to other people." This is how he put it, looking back, in an interview in 2020 for *The New York Times*—because, he thought, "my stuff is too unorthodox." He considered Coltrane's approach more widely transferrable. And indeed Coltrane's influence can be heard throughout the jazz of succeeding generations of musicians. Rollins's work—and working out what this meant was the work of his notebooks—was something else.

3

There is a turn towards the spiritual in Rollins's notebooks over the late 1960s and into the '70s that is not unlike the new spirituality in Coltrane's music, starting with *A Love Supreme* (1965), or the work of, say, Pharoah Sanders or Yusef Lateef. The entries also grapple with more abstract concepts. In one passage he records the way that, "after *hearing a firm definite tone*," his "consciousness" was able "immediately ... to *discern the octave* and 'pick it out of the air into the instrument' so to speak." His descriptions of sound are no longer just immanent but numinous.

In one passage, for instance, Rollins writes: "It happened that the lights being brite caused after-images and sensations which helped by a small auditorium and backstage gave effectual visualization. A move towards one object envisioned—a turnback of apprehension and I was engaged in one movement while playing. *I dreamed with the music.*" This "realization" took place during his first tour of Japan, an event that had a profound impact on both his music and his writing. Inspired by conversations with Japanese musicians and priests, he supplemented his ongoing research into the history of reed instruments and flutes with observations on two traditional instruments, the hichiriki and shakuhachi. Rollins was already interested in Zen Buddhism and Hindu mysticism before the tour, but while he was in Japan he was introduced to an eclectic mixture of the two: Oki-do, a practice developed by the eccentric yogi Oki Masahiro. Rollins stayed and studied with him for an extra two weeks at the end of his time in Japan. Oki's syncretic teachings brought together elements of Zen, Chinese Daoism, and Indian yoga; his practical emphasis on breath and tendency towards conceptual synthesis suited Rollins perfectly.

During these decades, Rollins's curiosity was as sharp as ever, and after his encounter with Oki, the scope of his personal research grew ever more wide-ranging: reading lists included books on auditory science and human biology. He studied philosophy and the history of black poetry, seeking recommendations from universities and poets, and his archive includes the recommended reading list for PhD students in anthropology at Columbia University. Even more suggestive are a selection of West African poems amongst his archives, including work by Léopold Sédar Senghor and David Diop, along with essays on these writers that Rollins had annotated. Rollins never sought to publish any of his notes as poetry, unlike his contemporary, the prolific poet Sun Ra. But it is hard to miss the poetic cadence and careful lineation that Rollins introduces now, and the following lines might well have sprung from Ra's Afrofuturist pen:

Inside of me
Songs of mystery
And then I see Nubia

Rollins and Ra did not just share an interest in drawing connections with African aesthetic traditions. Both men shared an esoteric taste in reading, and like Ra, Rollins was particularly interested in Rosicrucianism. His notebooks contain quotes from the Bhagavad Gita, the great Hindu epic, and later muse on the possibility that he and his wife share a kind of ESP. These were not new tendencies, in and of themselves. It seems totally natural to find Rollins interested in the fact that Pythagoras and Siddhartha Gautama (the Buddha) were contemporaries. But when he writes that "a great musician must be a man of great spiritual status" like "ascetics and yogis or disciples of great saints," he is going beyond his earlier belief in cultivating a holistic identity.

Rollins's interest in both yoga and Zen has a certain connection with the general tendency towards spirituality in jazz, but they have less bearing on his music than they do on his life. The notebooks reveal someone invested in these both as daily practices and as ways of understanding his relationship to the world. Over this period entries track his progress with different positions—he notes at one point that he "can now do the lotus pose fairly well, even though I have missed practice often"—and increasingly, his notes appear on bespoke stationary. The header, "The Sonny Rollins 'Yoga for Americans' Club," signaled his ambition to promote the practice; his notes include a draft letter to "Mr. Oki," explaining that "plans for the Yoga group are coming along much better than one should hope for." Although these plans never amounted to much more than the stationary, Rollins kept in touch with his "mortal teacher and guru." He made trips to India to further his training and continued to practice yoga for the rest of his career.

On several occasions during these years Rollins took a sabbatical from performance as he had in '59, no doubt at least partly in response to a larger crisis in jazz over this era. He began to experiment with electronic instrumentation—and not just the electric guitar and bass but Moog synthesizers, too—and he was hardly alone in this; Miles Davis had begun to play around with electric instruments as early as *Filles de Kilimanjaro* (1968), and Herbie Hancock and Sun Ra both started including Moogs around the same time as Rollins. But where his conceptual and perceptual inquiries continued to yield some real successes, incorporating a wider range of accompaniments only amplified Rollins's own uncertainties about the quality and style of his performances. There are several notes that address this "musical identity crisis," as Rollins started to imagine it, and almost all of these are associated with less traditional jazz instruments, like "sounds induced from Moog." His response was not immediate, but increasingly he found that unaccompanied solos offered the creative freedom (and confidence in his identity) that he had been searching for. Early observations that he needed "some private moments—more perhaps unmiked Rollins—personal Rollins—intimate etc." suggest a trajectory his concerts would follow for the rest of his career. Rollins found ways to make the exploration of his time away the substance of his performance. He puts it most clearly when he affirms: "I am a *singular* artist. I do a singular thing." For the first time, his notes start to take on a retrospective voice, actively taking stock of his legacy.

The style and content of the notebooks from the '70s vividly convey Rollins's moments of uncertainty. One can hear a keen sense of crisis in the tone of throwaway notes, as much as in prolonged reflections. On one practice sheet, Rollins writes to himself: "This is no laughing matter." He ends another passage with the rather equanimous observation "things are never constant"—before sharply veering into pessimism: "Disaster is coming. Disasters are coming." In many of his notebooks from the bridge years, Rollins had addressed himself directly, giving himself advice, or reminding himself of rules that he had decided on before. His tone could be firm, his language always direct, but he was rarely overtly critical of himself. The strictness and occasional tough love of those earlier notebooks, now turns to harsh self-critique: "As I look in mirror—too much fat ass." Other comments reveal an earlier history of (sometimes violent) frustration with his own failings; in one particularly moving note he contemplates showing his wife, Lucille, "how I fucked up my own nose making it more bulbous. A way of hurting myself because of my guilt feeling re: my musical inefficiencies."

In his self-critique, as in reflections on ascetics or the disciples of mystics, Rollins was searching for a way to measure greatness that qualified musical talent in non-worldly terms. Right from the start, his writing had reflected his drive to produce the best music that he could. To do things as well as they could be done. But increasingly his notes show a need to imagine what it means to do things well that does not rely on either the immediate response of an audience or the slower-burning commercial response of the market. There is something moving and essential in the way he frames this in another note, ahead of a meeting with his friend Charles Mingus. He writes, "Ask Charles: is it about eating and putting a roof over your head? Is that what life amounts to? Or 'Is that *all* life is about,' correctly put." With hindsight, as in a 2005 interview in *Jazz Times* with fellow saxophonist Joshua Redman, Rollins could identify the early 1970s as another watershed in his career. His decisions were no longer "about the money."

It is striking to read Rollins describe himself, in notes from 1973, as "old" and "tired." He was forty years old and—as it turned out—not even halfway through his career. It was another thirty-five years before he finally wrote a note to himself, saying "Maybe think about retirement when listening to my playing (technically) at this point," and even then, he found that his playing still met his own standards for another four years. His last concert would be in 2012. But as Redman observes, some of Rollins's first recorded performances were from before he turned twenty, and his breakthrough albums were cut in his early twenties, when he "had been playing the saxophone for less than ten years." Already, Redman points out, Rollins was "playing on the highest level imaginable." He was "an absolute prodigy." In that interview, Rollins agreed and admitted that, as the '70s progressed, his early success began to feel like a "burden," and he felt "the weight of the '50s...more than at other times." One response was to limit his performances; in keeping with his renewed emphasis on motives, he became much more selective about how and why he played.

But his notebooks reveal another response, which distinguishes the latter half of his career: For the first time, Rollins began to reflect consciously on his legacy. Perhaps the clearest distillation comes when he writes,

> For the past 40 years Sonny Rollins has been making and remaking jazz history, day by day. One of the most inventive improvisors in the history of music. There is the feeling that the truly great artists are gone—Parker, Ellington, Armstrong, Young, Holiday, Tatum, Miles, Coltrane. Rollins is the last remaining Titan, encompassing all of the great stylistic and technical innovations of the post–World War II era.

Placing himself within both a specific cultural moment and a longer lineage, Rollins was able to take stock of his career in a way that, until now, had run counter to his own philosophy. So long as he was busy "making and remaking jazz history," he could not afford to dwell on past successes. But in his later decades, Rollins derived a certain kind of peace from this retrospective vantage point. It allows him to "deduce" an "intelligent purpose behind life which (as long as I strive for perfection and am honest with myself) is a positive, nurturing, nourishing immutable essence." Once he had discerned a point of continuity, he could accommodate the ups and downs of his career as natural parts of a coherent and, ultimately, positive life.

4

In the early 1950s, when Rollins first began to keep notebooks, jazz writing was a limited field. The folk history of jazz, and many of its most important symbols, had been brought together in the seminal 1939 book *Jazzmen*, but serious historical and critical attention only came later in the '50s. Autobiographies also began to appear in the late '50s and early '60s, starting with Billie Holiday's *Lady Sings the Blues* (1956) and Sidney Bechet's *Treat It Gentle* (1960). Like *Jazzmen*, both "autobiographies" were works of multiple hands, involving ghostwriting and recorded conversations and full of mythologizing and flamboyance. This was taken to an extreme by Rollins's friend and correspondent Mingus. His sprawling autobiography, *Beneath the Underdog* (1971), was widely criticized for what was seen as a crass exploitation of stereotypes of jazz culture that at times verged on sexism and racism. While more moderate biographies (like Duke Ellington's 1973 *Music Is My Mistress*) and increasingly vivid and thoughtful liner notes emerged through the '60s and '70s, jazz writing continued to suffer from a mixed reputation.

Rollins's notebooks stand out both for their function—written for personal use, and best understood as a record of his thoughts in motion—and for their style. Unlike retrospective books or interviews, they are not subject to the distortions of memory or later preoccupations. Neither does Rollins write to fit a preexisting arc. There is no heroic trajectory here; he is painfully honest about difficulties and shortcomings even at the height of his professional success. All the same, these notebooks resist the work of diaries, rarely offering insight into day-to-day experiences. In fact, taken as a whole, it is the opposite that stands out: Rollins's tendency to synthesize and distill. A habit that began as a means of sustaining a period of renewed dedication to doing things well, where reflection would allow him to evaluate his own success and calibrate routines, gradually became a lifelong commitment.

The most profound and moving passages, to my mind, are those moments where Rollins achieves an aphoristic concision and clarity. They feel all the more moving because they genuinely helped Rollins himself. After his bridge years, he returned to the world to cut one of the most enduring records of his career; continuing writing, he was able to maintain his own high standards of performance for more than forty years—in the face of peers passing, or giving up, or telling him that he should quit. But, as Rollins closes one of his last notebooks, "No matter how you feel, get up, dress up, and show up."

The Bridge Years

MOTIVES AND AIMS

The idea of "teaching" music in the prescribed manner is our attempt to present people with a view of that finer side of their nature which is akin to such things as trees, grass, sky, among other natural phenomena.

It is this appreciation of and uniting with such things which determine our ability to establish a "contented" existence in the world of finance, business, economic security etc. This is why the ventures of the project must always uplift and inspire people.

They must come away inspired and uplifted from any contact with PROJECT.

In order to bring such inspiration to people I must not be concerned with applause by the audience. I must stand erect, tall, and straight. I must be of a clear head and pure heart (no stimulants).

I should not be either pleased or despondent over a performance and/or solo—always rather directing my attention to the SOUND of the music, and in this way what is produced will assume its subsidiary nature to what my intent and ideal is. In this way I will be doing my part to inspire and uplift the congress of people who "came to see."

Man is the highest expression of the spirit-formed mass of cells touched by the positive quality of nous. There are other such entities in the universe, such as animals, who are like man a combination of cells functioning as a unit of spirit-created form, impregnated with the vital life force. Plants are likewise a negative spirit mass who breath in positive vital life force (thru stomata?).

Daily exercise
U.R. Upright rowing
B.B.P. Behind back press
F.R. Forward raise
M.P. Military press
B.O.R. Bent over rowing
S.U. Sit-ups (do at least 25 at all times)
L.E. Leg extensions (do at least 30)
Kindly remember that when carrying or working out with the dumb-
    bells—ALWAYS CARRY THE SHOULDER HIGH

That interval between 3rd c and 5th-6 and/or 3rd up to tonic; the interval of a-b can be more easily conceived when thought of as a 3rd up to its tonic—eliminating the "bogus" of the "'minor 6' arithmetical equation," with its past fears and imagined difficulty.

Your beautiful collaboration with Thelonious is indeed worthy of the highest commandment from this individual it receives that.

After hearing the record today, it was the necessary, proper, and right thing to so inform you.

Continued success in and throughout life.

Sincerely,
Sonny Rollins

Lip Muscle Exercises:

While holding the left (come right down from your heart and lift hand to the mirror's left side) upper lip in high up (pulled up position) move and maneuver lower lip + related muscles (along its circumference and along the sides of mouth) up to where upper lip and other muscles can be safely as stilled as these are lower.

Put tongue on mouth roof—close the teeth—raise lower or rather upper left side of upper lip.

The bottom teeth should not "jut" out beyond their position when together and you must keep them always in proper position by #1 placing tongue on roof, #2 raise left upper lip, #3 bring teeth in together in "bite rest" (not too hard!), #4 (while keeping all three) operate lower teeth down, up, down, up, down, up. Remember the top is stationary.

You can't start at G and go down, you gotta start at G and go up!!

Hindu Music
6 Ragas (basic)

Raga: a progression of tones having as a minimum number of said tones the amount of 5 tones as a minimum (to constitute a RAGA)

The notes or tones are broken up thusly into these everyday counterparts...

"the leading note" or KING

"a secondary note" or PRIME MINISTER

"helping notes" or attendants

"a dissonant note" or the ENEMY

To determine which E♭ or C is meant by the designation we will play on our instruments, the equation based upon every E♭ or C playable and in so doing no doubt soon find the particular pitch note originally intended.

Maybe even a mental playing can determine where the pitch of the designate tone is.

"Designate Tone" then refers to the first tone of any equation.

"Reconstruction Era as it led to a setback in Negro advancement"

—please check the truth of this above.

Check current percentage not allowed (NEGRO) to vote as of now.

The proposed skin (drum or tambourine) over the bell for modification purposes could be tied with cat gut, around the bell, to be kept taut and firm and to hold same in place.

Rule 1:
When riding in any vehicle of a motor-driven nature (cars, trains, buses etc.) it is advisable to arrange breathing so that an exhale will always coincide with the stopping of said vehicle. Hold out exhale!
    Reason? —fumes.

On all melodies, after playing a phrase and reaching for a breath, always start the next phrase more softly then build up volume through succeeding phrasing—especially on "ballad/bottom of horn" type melodies.

It is important to be versed in what has preceded in the evolution of the Jazz Movement. So Rascher says when he says that the artist must be able to reproduce.
    It seems that Mr. Rascher is in this opening paragraph on pg 8 referring to the interpretation of a piece of repertoire by a performing artist, as he himself does today. There is however a link or chord which makes the above conclusion equally applicable in improvised music.

Check into a life-size skeleton frame—where one can be obtained.

The instantaneous creation of music—an unbroken link from thought to thing—immediately—at once—intelligently—but with emotion.

A person who is punctual about keeping an appointment is demonstrating firstly a certain control over himself, with a certain ability to command circumstance, or to direct circumstance, or to act upon rather than being acted upon.

A person who keeps an appointment punctually is demonstrating a control which while beginning with himself, reaches outward to include anything with which he comes into contact.

If we are to discuss punctuality we must determine whether one is willfully and consciously late or whether one is genuinely late— more or less beyond his control.

As if to confirm my understanding of whether or not a note can be different and yet the same—I listened to the overtone ring from the Grand Piano as it responded to my notes.

I discovered that many variations of an (in tune) note produce different amounts of vibrations—thus producing different sounds (or tones). I played 3 alternate fingerings of the same note.

All of the fingerings produced a note (or tone) that was in tune, by virtue of the fact that they each made the (A♭) or rather piano

G♭ ring out, but each one produced a ring of more or less vibrations which accounted for the different overtones achieved.

On the piano "touch" (which must be considered a better term than anything pertaining to volume) is the equivalent of the auxiliary fingerings (also called alternate fingering or "fake" fingering) of the wind and other than well-tempered instruments.

This time I produced the note F. C was being played and F was being thought of. Could Rascher mean this or imply such creation?

Could the rule be that since D produces an F♯ in its 5th partial, an F♯♯ (fingered) produces a D?

YES—I have now so proven

Now to see if this implies and bears out what I think . . .

"The Night Club"

The working conditions of many great jazz musicians are very, very far . . . below par! I myself am beginning to acquire a great dislike of them. This is especially true now that I can see them as a customer. What we have is this: the owners of these clubs are generally not only ignorant of good music but morally opposed to its promulgation. While they want the money jazz brings them, they don't want integration of white and colored (of course a certain amount of that is inevitable). They don't want to respect an artist, as they really have no education for the finer things. They are by and large a group of "shady characters" closely associated with underworld elements and figures.

The result is that the poor innocent musician is not allowed to

9

operate in a friendly conducive atmosphere, something which I daresay is of infinite importance, albeit to some more than others. Also children are not allowed as indeed they should not be. But how then are they to see and listen to this wonderful music? Also there is here the whole question of the stigma, which connects itself as a result of the incompatible marriage of jazz and nite club.

Now please don't ask me yet for my solution to the problem, but I am working on it. I venture to say it is inextricably tied to the other studies to which I am vowed. My music must solve these problems not so much for me alone, but for the coming human being (I hope I can be allowed to include little Theodore in this group). Yes, my friend, jazz music is a tremendous power for good. As indeed is all music which is enjoyed by people, but I think especially jazz! Not only is there unlimited space (as in the universe) to explore in jazz, but it also embodies and can capture within its framework all of the other musics of the world. Yes, jazz is a free planet where everything is happiness and love. It fills everyone's need for something stable to cling to in this world (on this planet) of changing appearances and material illusion, for in jazz all conflicts are resolved, all people recognize and adhere to this universal tongue. Jazz is the personification of music. It should then be accorded the presented respect it must occupy to be made potent for its service to mankind.

The motive for doing a thing is inevitably and ultimately ABOVE that thing.

Today when accent playing D♭, first hit with left hand G + D♭, then with right hand the remainder or C (all bottom 4 right-hand fingers).

To continue: on E♭ accent playing first hit all of left hand (as with D♭ above) with right pinky E♭ simultaneously—then close down the 3 right-hand fingers of D.

A♭ would be left + right pinky A♭ E♭ first then G.

On G hit left-hand G with right pinky, and accent with F♯.

Do not forget the first finger right hand which remains down from high A♭ up to at what I play now as Eb the upper switch here would then occur from high G to A♭.

Today:

Come up at once. Stop…breathe…go down.

Stop…breathe…come up.

This can develop style as well as prevent embouchure change (forced by lack of air) when reversing and going in the opposite direction of that which said phrase began in.

Persevere I shall.

Manifesting itself as an "outside" material sound—

I am turned on, so to speak, and attuned as if started reasoning clearly, as my body becomes imbued with the physical energy necessary to carry thru the dictates of my consciousness. Perhaps these sounds which I hear are only changed in as far as my conception of it is concerned and they consequently are not more pronounced in their reality as I have said. But it must be remembered that I am aware of the constant din of sound firstly; secondly is that out of this din there is one sound which supersedes all and strikes out from the din though it be returning to its normal part of the din. The fact that one of these and other sounds will become momentarily pronounced as a normal and regular behavior pattern of the day does not either negate any influence I here make as I am aware of all factors concerned here.

Just at that time I am awakened through the medium of one of these sounds which might be described in most cases as distracting in natural sounds.

Someone said "the easiest way is not always the best way." Although no doubt this quotation was well intentioned it is in fact only half correct. In truth and in all practical application . . . the easiest way is the best way.

Deep breathing must be considered in the light of its many therapeutic values.

By not allowing your lungs to go through this process one is first and foremost doing something drastically different to good breathing.

Well, what then is good breathing, what do you mean when you say "good breathing"?

Well, I mean by good breathing the ability to pull power up from your lungs with the velocity and control you deem necessary.

While smoking cigarettes I found the following things to be true:
a) I felt a general depression of spirit
b) a general tiredness of body
c) a dark brown stain on my thumb and forefinger (on nail and fingertips)
d) sharp pains similar to indigestive pains in chest area*
e) a shortness of breath through the inability to breathe deeply
f) a restlessness without purpose, a nervous exhilaration with a strong feeling of defeat seeming inevitable

To Find:
Atlas of Human Anatomy for the Artist, Stephen Rogers Peck

Vowels:
EE (like in bee)
A (like in glass)
Ou-O (like in water)
O (like home)
Ö (like in flirt or the French "fleur")
Ü (like in Debussy)

*These pains go back to youth before smoking, so cannot be attributed to nicotine alone. I cannot deny however that nicotine must surely be aggravating a condition chronic.

13

"Impulse"
Obeying an impulse. Relaying the sound of the inner voice.

Possible Book:
First Rules for Saxophone
First Saxophone Rule Book
Saxophone Rules
First Book for Saxophone
Saxophone First Rules: A Student Guide

Making A♭ you must think left hand—or left-hand G, if you prefer.

In preparation of playing, the first action is the putting on of the strap! Make whatever adjustments of strap necessary. Adjust neck position. Release all pads which may be stuck. Align mouthpiece. Determine what note you will commence with and what style bite you will use.

Today: Playing sequences which utilize middle D (side), de-emphasize this note, almost skipping it entirely while running around it.

Breathe up, high back. This will pull you down lower. This amounts to a stronger exhale motion; a pulling exhaling should result, up into the lungs and back.

Always remember that time is relative to the amount of concentrated thinking—in any endeavor.

Today: Continue to stress the "C emphasis" (as in low B♭), to low B. This, rather than the D for low B emphasis.

I attempt to picture in material form the shape created by my sense vibrations when playing notes. Tone also plays a part in this incomplete depiction.

In motion simultaneously are: 1. fingering with emphasis; 2. same size embouchure; 3. breathing; 4. etc. etc. Rather than confine, this enables mind to be free to think, having completed the "menial" tasks, so to speak.

Strict observance must now be shown to eating of non-liquid foods plan. I believe that the energy expended through the digestive function is detrimental to my health. I must consequently adhere strictly to the liquid diet for which I have already made readiness.

On going down from low C B B♭, minimize the left pinky stretch to the brass-most part of the key in favor of the new concept of a more straight down from B to B♭ manipulation. This straight up and down fingering is best exemplified when ascending from B♭ to B etc. on upward.

Also, today when exercising always first hit other pads then hit accent of all notes. This is perhaps the most important step to date in the "accent lessons."

When contemplating on smoking followed by sucking up same occurs, it is then time to stop and save remainder—immediately.

Chromatic scale must be played accenting every other note.

Among things which must be observed daily is breath-blow exercise. This leads to a sort of double tongue-ing effect when done faster—e.g. B♭ would be hit more or less open and accented; B would be closed up by tongue; and so on chromatically up.

The importance of the Joyce shoulder is twofold (at least) in that it permits deep breathing, being in truth the only way to take a real deep breath or to maintain breathing which will enable you to either take a deep breath or a series of short ones or hold a breath etc.
    In other words the Joyce shoulder must be used!
    B♭ should be stressed in the trill position for all (low) B♭ work

rather than the attack position; you must curve that pinky and get the best B♭ at that position.

The universe is constantly in motion.

In playing B♭ scale please play B♭ thinking of C as efficiently as you play C thinking of G. For one thing to facilitate this action, keep stressing the accent notes (G and C) with force when coming to them.

Also, when playing B♭ scale up to middle C and back always, after reaching low B♭, strike B♭ again (or twice in a row) when repeating the scale. Also, think right for B♭, left for C.

This Golden Rule
We must obey
Always end a phrase of playing
In its perfected corrected way

In making the connection between middle octaves chromatically, be sure to think left pinky from A♭ to C, and when making C strike the B♭ key much more pronouncedly. Guard against embouchure change while making the connection.

Insufficient wind intake will not allow a tone to be hit and sustained without tone variation upon the attack; therefore, for the sustaining of tones (and other playing as well), take a deep breath thru the nose. This breath should be pronounced and audible, at least for the present.

Be sure not to breathe in through the mouth and (also what is incorrect) up through the horn, but always through the nose—audibly. This automatically makes you tighten your grip on the mouthpiece and thus sustain embouchure.

Also, play a phrase out of breath before taking in more wind through the nose.

Be sure when following stomach-out breathing principle to play the note while stomach is out.

Practice this.

Equality:

The right to be able to do what you ought.

Not biological, but equal opportunity to realize individual potential.

To Read:

Physical Basis of Music, A. Wood (Macmillan Co.)

Musical Acoustics, Charles Culver

Sensations of Tone, Helmholtz (Dover)

Musical Engineering, Olson (McGraw-Hill)

Sept. 8, 1960

Birthday now past but tendencies toward disruption still exist. So I have not fought my desire to violate dietary Truths, which I have painfully come first to realize and most recently to actuate. Rather I have given them their head—also I have not dwelled on my other problem rather having given in to the urge which I felt strongly last night.

My point is that by the very documenting of these transgressions I am demonstrating my awakening strength which will come into full bloom at such time as I have suffered through the various manifestations of these problems.

And yet even as I struggle with the exact same problems can I deny a greater awareness of them and the feeling that they will be "conquered" more through time and understanding gradually, than a pointed effort to "break" an unnecessary habit.

And so patience and understanding is the word.

The violin has four strings which are tuned in perfect 5ths by adjusting the tension by means of the pegs—and are made to give the various notes of the scale by stopping (e.g. pressing) them with the finger down onto the fingerboard—and so shortening their vibrating length.

In air waves, the waves travel at the rate of 1 mile every 5 seconds; thus, the eye cannot actually see these waves.

Sensations from a "musical wave" or tone are differentiated from noise by the regular frequency of the waves. Noise waves or sounds are of a discontinuous order. Musical sound waves are equally spaced. Noise sound waves are irregularly spaced.

Greek early music was separated into a series of seven modes which can be fairly imitated on a modern pianoforte by playing scales beginning respectively on E, F, G, A, B, C, D without using any of the black keys.

Half attack and half breathe-blow lower tones as well as upper ones (where you first designed the method as a way of better toning the extreme upper register).

Don't deviate from one idea to another while practicing—in other words, when you hit upon something that needs doing and you are receptive to doing this, stick on that. Don't, in the course of doing it, get side-tracked into another area which at the time has no relation. Of course they will both ultimately show their relationship—but at this particular time, do not deviate from one thing to another.

Hunch-raise left shoulder high to bring freedom to lungs.

Indeed, victory is ahead—but do not forget that included in that "ahead" are many patient, slow, painstaking efforts. It seems to be very far away today...that "ahead."

Perhaps because of a long practice session yesterday?

Definitions:

Auscultation—listening to the abdomen or chest to determine condition therein—also listening to any other surrounding part—neck etc.

Breathing: the inhalation and exhalation of air respiration.

Abdominal or diaphragmatic in which the inspiratory movement is chiefly downward, the depression of the diaphragm thus causing the abdomen to expand during inspiration.

Cog wheel: a jerky interruption of the breath sounds. Heard at times by auscultation.

Paradoxical breathing—deflation of the lung during inspiration, and inflation of the lung during the phase of expiration.

The lung therefore inflates when breathing in. The diaphragm depresses downward when breathing in. The diaphragm depression causes the abdomen to expand when breathing in.

Abdominal respiration: effected mainly by the action of the diaphragm, the movement being chiefly of the abdominal walls.

Abdomen: the body cavity bounded by the diaphragm above and the pelvis below.

Playing a D scale:

Play D E F♯ then after pause at F♯ connect G A B C♯ D.

When descending pause at F♯ and attack E so as to facilitate the movement from F♯ to E.

Playing a B♭ scale be sure to keep your left hand properly positioned. In other words only your pinky should move when you are attacking B♭ from above or starting an ascent from B♭ the other three fingers must be securely in place for the other notes. They must not sag down toward B♭ with the pinky as you have been doing.

When running B whole tone scale pause at F, attack G cleanly thru octave, and repeat as necessary.

Play low B up to E. Keep left pinky as near to D♭ as possible* when playing B. When making E the left pinky will go across to D♭ in an *easy natural progression*. This will eliminate *blind spots* such as is often encountered in that area.

It is becoming apparent that I hear naturally a sort of dissonance based upon 7 keys harmonizing together. These harmonies have been previously investigated in the "change of key" exercises I often play (on particular songs; changing keys at different parts of the melody) and prior to this on the E against C harmonies I was led to investigate by virtue of Bird. Now it seems I am hearing three different keys simultaneously.

Learning
When practicing yesterday I found it extremely difficult to execute certain passages which I had previously (the day before) seemed to

---

*Left pinky must strike the black part of the B key, in other words.

have accomplished. This demonstrates that we must be able to do a given thing over a given period of time before that thing reaches the point of understanding referred to as learning.

All people pass through yearly, monthly, + daily cycles during which they react differently to the same stimuli. We observe this and say that we feel good or bad, not being able to understand or control these conditions. It should be pointed out here that we are referring to "good + bad feelings" exclusive of some discernable physical illness which could also produce such statement of feelings. To go on, what happened to me was that I executed the passages at a time when I felt "good." The next day when I felt not so good I could not so readily execute this passage—although after continuous reiteration of same I regained the proficiency which I had previously exhibited.

Therefore when one had learned something (as walking) one can do this thing at any period of one's cycle. As one walks every day regardless of one's "feelings."

A proclivity for impatience is by far the most serious problem confronting me in my work.

Slow and or fast are illusory conditions in that they are relative to comprehension. When one comprehends one can execute as one desires. Naturally in order to comprehend one must go "slowly." But as I have said it is a misnomer to refer to the detailed concentration of any given exercise as slowly. One is after all not going slowly but deliberately and comprehensively.

Status terms
1. Egocentric-familistic
   small, isolated groups
2. Sociocentric familistic
   many large family groups
3. Egocentric non-familistic
   bureaucratic society—lords, vassals, serfs etc.
4. Sociocentric non-familistic
   many terms non-personal like doctor

Blow only open (no attack tones)
1. Don't attack when exercising in and around G (F, F♯, G, A♭, A).
2. Remember Joyce shoulder for breathing (deep breathing) if not for anything else . . . utilize it.
3. A danger point to be stressed is middle C to D♭ to D to E♭ and on back down past D♭ to C to B. This approximate area as well as the G area* are to be stressed for the purpose of not attacking or changing embouchure when playing in them.
4. Right hand must remain still and firm when coming up from B♭ to B to C etc. Right pinky must subsequently stretch down to the low C key and maintain a more sure firm grasp, not to move when going down to B + B♭.
5. Do not eat food in a cramped position as the indigestion resulting is often acute.

*henceforth called G area + C area.

Whole Blow from low B♭ up

Instead of spitting out notes, open blow with the added bite effect
    of tongue hitting reed bottom.

Gradually remove tongue from reed as note is brought out.

Make B, think D (low).

Make C, think G (low C).

Make (low) B♭, think low C.

Going from: G down C, think right-hand G left or G for C.

On making low D, think left hand and/or D♭ key accent!!

On low E, accent first 2 fingers of right hand.

Another good day to think and be thankful for.

Peaceful morning with a new resolve to maintain peace and tran-
quility without the encumbrance of an insidious habit (cigarettes).

Benny took me to his tailor to complete my alterations and con-
versed upon the racial scene as it exists for entertainers around this
(Gold Coast) section of Chicago.

I must try to desist from lusting after women.

I must remember that events are happening for the good—and
not to get disillusioned when I fail to adhere to an ideal goal which
I set.

Even if there are more brilliant "jazz" (in the modern interpretations
of the word) artists and innovators among the "Negro race" (in the
modern interpretation of the word) this in no way contradicts the
quasi-racial nature of jazz, and mustn't we start speaking of MUSIC
and not jazz. Cannot this be the same principle by which people

are deluded into divisions. Divisions which are treacherously mis-leading, by their external manifestations. Who can deny that the greatest of any music is of a one-ness which transcends period, style, country, etc. It is the same line of reasoning which separates people on the basis of their physical impressions (manifestations). The point to be absorbed here is that any definition which seeks to sep-arate Johann Sebastian Bach from Miles Davis is defeating its own purpose of clarification. Thus we shall now hereafter and henceforth integrate if you will the word jazz into the word music. Yea as we strive, so mote it be.[1] The Musings of Miles is then the Bouncing of Bach both played against each other.

Sensing and discerning faults in men. Many of these faults are the faults which I myself am striving to (and which I have oh so recently) overcome. Thus I find myself succumbing to their way of thought. But why should I? One must aspire to the level at which one shall have completely and conclusively been convicted in the thought so as to be able to walk into the lion's den and demonstrate one's MAS-TERSHIP. For are you not then acting in concert and with the approval of the Divine Essence?

Jazz is the embodiment of the American Ideal spawned by various ethnic cultures given any opportunity for expression in America. Jazz is a vigorously hybrid product which is All American. Therefore great care should be taken not to synonymize Negro and Jazz and not to depict Jazz as a Negro product.

It is in reality the music of America created by Americans for the edification of all of mankind.

Today

Before commencing to play always follow these rules:

A. hunch left shoulder into position

B. start fingering with cheeks contracted

C. produce first tone with cheeks extracted as fingering and breathing assume their functions properly

Breakthru:

The soreness in mouth is agitated and maybe results from my changing of cheek position while playing instead of keeping cheeks out.

Start thinking of A♭ as G accenting G or 4th finger left hand (next to pinky).

Try to eliminate the habit of playing down to low B♭ and stopping. By letting less and less air in down to B♭ you are adhering to the incorrect method. Consequently from now on: never end any sequence of playing on low B♭ always come back up, either actually tone-ing or "finger breathing." Never stop on B♭!!

Use tongue on reed for low B♭–B–C etc. As well as cheeks and stomach out as well as C B♭ B etc.

Today—

It will be henceforth emphasis on this principle in regards to low tones. a) Always attack with cheeks puffed out in a sort of spitting way, by this I mean the tongue on reed method as revealed on this page other side; b) always keep in mind which hand is being emphasized by "finger vibrato" to come after note has been attacked and held briefly. Please to cease playing chromatic runs down to low B♭ and stopping as prescribed on back of page!!!

Clamp down hard on low B when hitting it so as to break in this note which appears to be a little weak as compared to her sister B♭.

When coming up from B♭ to B watch out for tendency to move the right hand. Note rather that the right hand does not move until D natural!!

Today:
Keep left pinky on brass, closer to you when playing low B.

When observing down to B♭ rule, carry into any sequence which must never end in short breath. Follow all such sequences with finger breathing.

On trilling G–B♭—accent one or the other.

Middle C must be hit by moving right hand slightly down, not by moving left and right!!

Keep left hand rigid and dip right side of hand to make all side Cs when ascending or descending.

Today—
Whenever finger breathing, always not only finger breath but swallow before bringing back tone sound.

Also, before starting to play always swallow first. Proceed slowly! When swallowing loosen up on mouthpiece bite.

Today

In general grip left hand tighter to keys, and hit B lower and closer to B♭ (low).*

Play whole tones on A♭ and G to determine correct placement of fingers.

The Harmonics:

It appears that on playing D and after obtaining an octave the next legible note is a perfect 5th or A. This is seen (at this time) to result in a perfect 4th or G. So one would then hear: 2 Ds, one A, and one G, simultaneously.

It has now been proven that B, C, D♭, D, E♭ can be played with octave and 5 (IIV) chromatically up. When starting on B lip for the 5th of each respective tone (key).

Start on low B♭ now. I hope this can be done right up the ladder. Do as many as possible. This is an excellent way to start any practice session as it accomplishes whole tone-ing while adding interest.

Always start on low B♭ and climb chromatically as far as possible.

Direction:

Today—from here in devote special attention to accenting notes as in series of 3 that you play in key of C.

*Left hand must be more strong + must turn even as right hand must in going from F♯ to E♭.

Today:

A) In playing any scales where you must switch off the D♭ key (middle G-A or low C to D) always hit the accent key hard. You can best illustrate this by playing a C major scale—when going from C to D, hit the D♭ key hard! (low C).

B) Also when playing a D-min scale keep going from F to G, hit the side F♯ or "accent key" very hard. This will facilitate easier movement; also accent D♭ when passing from G to A (on A).

C) When coming down on a D minor scale hit the G and the F harder than their respective accent keys.

D) When playing a C scale finger side C with knuckle of forefinger rather than finger itself.

E) When coming down from middle G♯ to C♯ (G♯ F♯ E D♯ C♯), hit your C key hard for a clear concise C♯. All other keys are in place—a strong C will produce a clear C♯.

Today:

Play E♭ scale up to E♭ above staff. Play this scale continuously; during breathing intervals continue to finger keys, then resume in meter the scale, at the point it was interrupted for breathing. Practice this as other exercises—slowly or fastly—make them correctly.

• This exercise draws attention to my evidently bad habit of taking a quick breath before hitting or attacking a note—don't forget, stomach out when breathing!

• A quick breath may be eliminated by keeping mouth on mouthpiece when breathing.

It now appears that the "quick breath" I refer to is nothing else but my taking my mouth off of the mouthpiece to breathe. Eliminate this habit now!! The fingers must consequently work independent of the breathing.

Today:
On going up to F chromatically or scale-wise try for the bottom 3rd of the middle finger to get proper key position. Incline hand on this note and favor it, at least temporarily.

Today:
STOMACH GOES OUT AS NOTE IS BLOWN—consequently instead of taking that breath before attacking, the breath becomes the first note.

Today:
STOMACH *OUT* WHEN BREATHING TODAY.

It is now becoming apparent that until a smooth manipulation is achieved in the G A F G F♯ G etc. area, lower tones and correct breathing are greatly hampered. Also note that when playing metal Berg keep horn high up on strap. This high strap produces a feeling of my tonsils coming together at some times. It is very much more like what should be happening I think. This also makes fingering easier!!

Perhaps this feels correct because it straightens up my posture.

In the playing of a whole E tone starting on E up to high E be sure to keep the left hand low so that it can make high D to E smoothly. The tendency here now is to hit D and E simultaneously instead of hitting D (going up). The dropping of the left hand thus reveals other benefits.

It appears side F♯ should be played as far toward hand of 4th finger as possible.

Today:

Check out theory: must coincide with normal smooth breathing. While fingering and breathing a note must always when played out, be played with cheek out. While only fingering and breathing it is assumed the cheek may maintain closed in position in accordance to whichever breathing position is best, and the "best" position for breathing while fingering is with cheeks closed; this also affords the benefit of resting embouchure while still carrying on the rest of it!!!

Also "standing about like Joyce" remember to keep the left shoulder held high.

From this moment on attempt to play everything as directed above. Let nothing else be considered valid (pay as you go principle) unless it contains the basis of playing above.

Today:

When playing side C or high E use the furthest most portion of the hand towards the hand, almost going into the upper palm.

Keep alert for position of middle finger making F and above, when using upper palm for high E as mentioned.

At this time it seems that the left elbow must be trained to remain free of the body while playing! Avoid contact and never lean elbow against body.

Today try to keep bigger bite in mind at all times.

Today going back to the use of palm for making side C + E as mentioned above. Strive to maintain this fingering position on both descending and ascending scales.

Today—cheeks must be puffed out at same degree when playing high or low C.

Keep same cheek puff through all playing!

Keep mouth on mouthpiece especially when ad-libbing don't forget to maintain a uniform cheek puff when changing octaves or when pausing to breathe.

Starts Mon.—1:00 PM—slow reading ? hour, but first do at least 5 min. whole.

Begin all practice sessions starting at 1:00 PM with 5 minute whole tone practice.

Note—practice can begin any day, time, or where but must commence at 1:00 PM for 5 minute whole and ? hour slow reading. This will be effective Mon. thru Fri.

Mon.—excellent if reluctant start and result—do not add on to schedule until Mon.–Fri. sessions are successful—at least 2 wks.

Tues. be very careful to play all so designated passages—slowly. The problem here is simple as it is complex. Once I play the doubtful passages slowly they become very easy and any mistakes are quickly ironed out. Once I play the same passages with no regard for time they appear difficult. Remember speed is relative, in that a thorough knowledge of a given passage will ultimately produce speed—so go slowly—

Wed. a) Henceforth lessons can begin anytime up to 1:00 PM—but no later. b) Spend 15 minutes on whole tones on days when tones lead into other channels. This way you can assure yourself of at least 5 minutes of only whole tones. c) On music go *slowly*!! Read C♭ ex. prior to playing it on horn!!

Thurs.—good practice session—continue.

Fri.—very good practice session—some liberties were taken with time—culminating nevertheless in a good session. Liberties must be taken but beware of too many of them—on Mon. emphasize once again a rigid 1:00 PM schedule.

Sat.

Sun. I discovered that I made a few squeaks when trying to play from upper register to lower register continuously or arpeggios up and down.

Wed. The weather has been unfavorable for me for so long now. Indeed it seemed to be interminable. Now the provinces that be have allowed us to once more breathe and feel the other side of nature. Remember this is it. This is the season, the reason for "makin' whoopee."

Thurs. Continuation of present policies. Great progress is being made. Today concentrate upon whole tones—slow reading—and thinking of G♭ as G♭ not as F♯ and of C♭ as that and not as B.

Sun.—cont. down the registers of the horn. These squeaks however shall only culminate in the next octave of the horn. They were not meaningless noise squeaks but rather seemed to be higher notes that I have not figured out yet. I should and will note here that this was brought about thru practicing of whole tones—whole tones in general as during regular Mon.–Fri. schedule and whole tones in particular by playing everything whenever possible.

Tues. Try to arrange time to return to original concept of late hour awakening activity as opposed to recent simultaneous early bed hours.

In some cases this might entail going out at night. You then must be sure not to defeat your cause by indiscriminate use of these out-door hours!!

Walking should be a good stimulant. If at first you don't succeed try to suck again.

In general not too bad.

Make up a chart for each day. Formulate a program built on what it is which we want.

Let the inside me be me.

Previously I had let the outside me designate the *real* me. The me of me. Me.

Now I shall let the inside me designate the real me and the outside me the OUTSIDE ME.

Invested with sanctity
(Schopenhauer)
Phenomenology
Ideologs
(Ide-a-logs)
Polemical

Geo-political
Mitigate
Metamorphosis

Antipathy
Antithesis

The order has been whispering to me at just such times as I would lose vision. Reaching me in a deeply personal revelation of a universal principle, testifying to the impersonality of character which I seek.

Sydney Smith as well as Emerson here contributed especially inspiring postulations, to name two.

Choose and discover which mouthpiece facing is best adaptable to the "stationary (more or less) bottom lip on reed in embouchure" position.

Which means, incidentally, which of my mouthpieces feel best playing in this manner. In other words, no parallel can be assumed valid as yet—but by finding any mouthpiece that works (which is the point) we can learn more about making valid statements about the matter.

Principle:
A fundamental truth or doctrine on which others are based. Rules of conduct or ethical behavior.

Questions:

The position of the tenor neck—does it matter? If so, is it more difficult to fill wind through such a shaped neck in distinction to the alto, baritone etc.?

Explain how sustained tones were used by me to practice lip control and hearing of note—leading to (thru strong hearing of tone) the very highest upper harmonics and a "series" of notes resembling the high flute notes of Japanese classical music. Is this the pure tune or pure sound referred to as the music of Greece long ago?

Take care of yourself.

Be pragmatic.

Knowledge never lets us down
When we seek it
(it is sought)
It will always be found

Knowledge never lets us down
Whenever we seek it
It will always be found

Knowledge never lets us down
If it is sought
It will be found

Knowledge has never let us down

To change plain breath into something which will in effect disperse itself in a uniformed and oscillating "wind wave" by vibrating at a faster rate than plain breath into a pipe can manage.

When you blow a breath of air or a breath stream into an instrument with such a vibrating transformer (reed) the stream itself is emitted in waves or vibrations.

Against I
An urge to smoke must be followed by concentration! Concentration on music should follow. If I smoke I then must concentrate as a penalty.

It is becoming increasingly clear that I must formulate a work schedule. There is no more need to be afraid of setting aside certain given times for study of certain subjects. Reading although being slowly carried out must be, I now believe, to a certain period of attention each day. There is no need to fear designation of a certain time to attend these studies as opposed to a program of regularity without time. Consider this and continue to work. Keep working on relationships between D + D♭–A + A♭–G + G♭–C + C♭.

Please be so kind as to begin consideration of regarding pills as an excuse and so begin considering termination of same. This was brought out to me through my associating health diet with same. Actually I must follow health diet while eliminating use of these medical pills which were at one time indispensable to me.

Indeed it should be made a point of that as much as I would like to have both smoking and health, it is an impossible task. It seems that nature will not compromise in this respect—why? Because "I know." It is the price of understanding.

There can be no doubt that smoking is for me physically and mentally wrong. It nevertheless has a small point made for it through the soul—(soulfully). This endorsement which my soul is reluctant to give keeps my soul divorced from my physical and mental however, and am I not after all seeking a union—a perfection—a meaningful purposeness towards which I may attune all of my faculties. Certainly it is clear that I need all of myself at my command in these provocative times.

Mon. Very good whole tone session which lasted much longer than my prescribed 5 min. By so practicing I found my chops too weak to successfully play my exercises—especially if I tried to attack each note slowly as I should be doing. I am bent at this stage to enlarge on my practice sessions. There is a danger inherent in changing too much of my schedule although perhaps if I keep my original schedule as a *minimum* amount of practice I might be successful in augmenting my program to suit my energy and conditions. I must however keep a minimum of ? hour on exercises at least and of 5 minutes whole tones at least. For instance right now I have stopped doing my exercises after about 15 minutes. I stopped as I stated because of tiring lips. I shall resume after and get in 15 more minutes at least—thereby amassing the proper time needed. On Tuesday tomorrow—once again blow whole tones on upper D, E, F etc. Facility is remarkably improved—keep in extra long whole tone session.

Tues. It is clear that my improvisational direction is still uncertain at this stage. Fair practice day—continue whole tone attack as practiced yesterday. Time which was spent on upper register soloing produced pressure on lip and also produced great tone potentialities —whole tone. Plus slow reading.

Wed.—a deviation from my usual schedule. A relapse—a time-wasting day—but then again I did get in another day of high note moving around and a little whole tones. I did not do very much reading however—hardly any. The day being one in which time passed very quickly I managed to get in a great deal of just blowing. I tried to incorporate whole tone attack to all notes whenever I thought of it and in general strengthened my lip with my upper register soloing and high note tone sustaining playing. The day was completed with my longest and most fruitful analyzation study. As if to compensate for the breaking of practice rules in the day I spent valuable time in analyzing—which should be done every day to some degree.

The sameness which has been implied between love + hate also applies between success + failure. What then appears to be opposite sides of the pole may in fact be just that but what must be stressed and what is usually overlooked is that both conditions are resident in the same pole. This then is to imply that these seemingly diverse conditions are in reality closely related.

Now let me begin by saying that many people who have succumbed to failure in one way or another have been just that close to success so as not to see it. And furthermore just a small extra measure of endeavor would have resolved this unreal juxtaposition for them and in their favor. The lesson to be drawn from this is in a practical way the lesson of perseverance, for we never realize how close we are to the positive expression of our endeavors or the "far end of our pole."

The sooner I face the startling and intriguing reality that there is within me a force working hard for my own destruction, even as I try to improve...

1961–1963

Fantastic Saxophone

A picture (photograph) of Manny's window for the first page/picture, showing the "gleaming, shiny, shimmering, bright, golden, curved, beautiful gleaming saxophones" to good advantage.

Boy, I wish I had one of those   and could play it too!

Now as if in answer—different print and location on page (of the following in distinction to the exclamation on previous page):

That's how "Sax Men" begin. For the first time they lay eyes on that curved shiny beautiful-looking piece of metal, it makes them feel proud and strong and important. Yes, important! If you had that sax you would really be somebody important. You would make people dance and be happy.

Yes, you can see yourself now, standing in front of those people and filling them with tones straight from your sax, handsomely groomed and dressed, horn gleaming like the sun as you perform in front of the crowds.

So you start playing the saxophone. Maybe not the one in the window, maybe even you just borrow one or use one.

Preparatory to playing:
Strap on first
Smile when playing for sound production

Titles:
The Fraternity of Saxophone
The Saxophone Fraternity
The Saxophone Brotherhood
Our Saxophone
Saxophone Energy and Health

Sonny Rollins and the "Pay as You Go" Method:
This method consists of stopping when you are ahead and afterwards successfully executing any given passage. Do not proceed with something new until every given passage is completely completed.

Titles:
Health and Music
Discovering the Saxophone
Fantastic Saxophone

My motivations in this matter are as follows:
a) A desire to disseminate proven principles as pertaining to the saxophone and those aspects of music which are indigenous to its mastery.

b) A desire to project an image which is necessary to balance and focus the true picture of the contemporary musician and more important to present to the young jazz student an example which can be exemplified in them without compromise of moral and/or religious principle.

c) A desire to touch upon those problems of being a professional which will come up during such situations as being on the road etc.

An attempt to stress clean living as a requisite to good musicianship and an attempt to unify these ideals so as to bring about the realization of the next American Dream, as it is vividly exemplified in jazz, which is a derivative music—comprising many elements, peoples, and countries.

To destroy the myths which separate not only jazz men of different ethnic backgrounds but indeed all men are plagued by this mistrust and misunderstanding based on fear and ignorance.

I shall attempt to bring this about solely by my dissertations on the saxophone and music in particular—touching upon the other matters with reserve and only when they particularly serve to illustrate a point. Let me add that everyday affairs are not so inimical to musical education as one might ordinarily think. To state one example: It had always seemed right and proper for jazz musicians to smoke cigarettes. The very few exceptions to this precept proved the rule. I have since discovered and learned to appreciate the fact that smoking is detrimental to the lung power and breath sustenance which one must employ to properly master the saxophone. As you can see I have already touched upon a subject of at least political and national significance: the smoking of cigarettes. To indicate further the treatment which should be accorded to subjects of this magnitude let me say that I will offer this advice only to saxophone players—not all.

I have always been humble and modest in my evaluation of myself and would not presume to attempt such a project did I not know that I am equally qualified to serve in this capacity. I bring with me the credentials gleaned from the breast of experience. I have indulged in all the vice associated with nite-club life and prevailed. I have learned my profession to a great extent by self-instruction. I have, in other words, grappled and overcome the things on which I will expand and will label proud truth as such as opposed to theory as such.

Musical Physics

A. Hearing the note. B. Hearing the first and last notes of the phrase as "part of the first note"! C. Roofed mouth.

When joining successive notes, note #2 is played from the same stream of air and embouchure position as note #1 employed. Note #3 is likewise fingered while the air stream and embouchure of note #2 is in effect. And so on—to create a ring on all notes and achieve "good intonation."

The tongue is resting upon (back upon) the mouth's roof. The further back, the more exercise is given to the throat area. Placing the tongue in a somewhat different posture would and can no doubt be beneficial to some other perhaps more subtle "working" in the region. All of this is where the *Fun of Exploring* comes in. So I won't and shan't spoil it by telling you or suggesting to you some particular result to expect. For my results may be different than yours and your results may be different from mine.

Sustained tones throughout.

The Importance of the Constant Smile
Smiling naturally by keeping a cheerful thought on the mind (a thought which would accompany a perennial smile; one of peace and happiness within should create this type of smile which is not to be confused with e.g. a laugh or a snicker, as in both instances a steady position of the mouth could not be achieved due to the irregular and excitedly jerky movements of laughing and/or snickering). What we want then is a natural smiling countenance which must not be too vigorous as in a laff, or too relaxed wherein the smile unless already practiced by you would not last too long—especially so as different thoughts may enter the mind at some point causing a more serious attention to what you are doing which of course causes the smile pose to become a more grim pose.

In the Tabernacle of Music
We come in, we put on our straps, we take out our horns, we begin to *hear our note*, we concentrate upon *our* note, and only when we find ourselves communicating through various musical statements which will occur simultaneously and in harmony with another sound from another horn do we become aware that there is another's activity present within our range of hearing. Then we let pure music take over and allow the higher more perfect language of creation to lead us into further avenues of harmony with those around us who do the same passive act of musical execution.

Pronouncements:
I. In playing B major scale left pinky must move from B to C♯ with-

49

out any right-hand movement. This will not interfere with the accentuation and mental image of C when making C♯.

In descending the B scale the image of E D C must be dominant—and at no time must you think of E D♯ C♯ fingering—although it is understood that E D♯ C♯ are the actual notes being produced. In other words the image must be of E D C as in a C major scale—thereby accenting the right hand and producing the correct manipulatory phenomenon. Do not disregard the proceeding no. II when practicing this B scale (the G for G♯).

NOTE: Every practice day during the month of April—touch upon each principle of this pronouncement.

II. Finger practice and practice chromatically ascending from B♭ up to the note (G) which puts into effect the common holding principle of the first section of this pronouncement. When so doing and reaching the F below that G be certain to direct the left pinky to strike the G♯ key and avoid the other surrounding keys. In this same context and regard for the upper region, daily practice this next lesson.

III. When coming down from high C always emphasize the *left-hand 4*—which finger is also emphasized for the following notes as low as A♭. Therefore always think left-hand 4 from A♭ up to E♭. Consciously practice left-hand 4 from E♭ or C down to Ab chromat. And then (*make the change to right-hand 3) for the G G♭ + F before hitting left-hand D♯ high for E, return to topic from E + repeat. This will not interfere with previous holding tone studies on A♭ G etc. as outlined in the first segment.

• When making change from A♭ to G the right-hand middle must be emphasized and synchronized, generally speeded up.

NOTE: In ascending chromatically up to G and beyond always

remember to accent G from the A♭ as outlined in the latter segment of the first segment. This G for A♭ is true for the 3rd A♭ as well as the first 2!

The sax can achieve any color within the orchestra. How often have I been fooled by its oboe-ish sound? And what a variety of tone it has displayed when simulating the sound of the trombone or the brilliance of the trumpet or the color that is open to us in the strings, brasses...

All of the tone colors which the different instruments achieve can be sounded on our saxophone. I have heard the sax achieve the quality of (to name just a few instruments) the trombone, the oboe, the clarinet, the bass, violin, the trumpet, the bassoon, the French horn, and some others as well. Such possibilities of expression are not to be found abiding in any other single instrument. And don't forget by the way that the saxophone has its own tone—generally different for each player, allowing that the individuality of the player should be brought out.

Tune this tenor pad-wise by:
Sounding the pads one step above the blown tone.
Further note: E♭ for low C; B for G on staff (treble).

There is today in existence a fraternity of people. People who were all irrepressibly drawn to the "horn of horns," "the instrument of instruments," the saxophone. Within its proportions we saw a better and more beautiful world. We saw, and see the means towards a better human being; towards the perfection of our selves.

Practice on horn all harmonic minor scales.

Lesson I: Intervals

An interval is the distance between two different notes. There are two types of interval, namely: harmonic and melodic. A harmonic interval is two notes played simultaneously. A melodic interval is two notes played one after the other.

Intervals used within one octave are:

Unison=same line or same space

2nd=line and space or space and line

3rd=two lines or two spaces

4th=two lines and a space or two spaces and a line

5th=three lines or three spaces

6th=three lines and a space or three spaces and a line

7th=four lines or four spaces

8th or octave=four lines and a space or four spaces and a line

There are two kinds of intervals: perfect and imperfect. The perfect intervals are octaves, unisons, 4ths, and 5ths. Perfect intervals are called perfect because they remain perfect when inverted—that is, placing the bottom note above the top note or visa versa. So a perfect octave becomes a perfect unison, a perfect unison becomes a perfect octave, a perfect 4th becomes a perfect 5th, and a perfect 5th becomes a perfect 4th.

Perfect intervals cannot be major or minor.

Perfect intervals widened ? step become augmented; perfect intervals lessened ? step become diminished.

Imperfect intervals: major, minor, augmented, diminished. These are called imperfect because they change qualities when inverted. Major becomes minor, minor becomes major, augmented becomes diminished, diminished becomes augmented.

Write all above intervals from any given note and name its quality, treble, and bass staff.

Lesson II: Chords
Chords are built up from a given root in thirds.
Triads:

      Major consists of major 3rd plus minor 3rd: 4+3

      Minor consists of minor 3rd plus major 3rd: 3+4

      Augmented consists of all major 3rds: 4+4

      Diminished consists of all minor 3rds: 3+3; dim. 7th: 3+3+3

      Exercise I: Construct major and relative harmonic minor scales in all keys up one octave, and construct triads up from each scale tone agreeing with the scale; number and name their qualities.

      Exercise 2: Practice all scales—full range of instrument up and down twice.

Lesson III: Connection of Chords thru Cycles
There are three cycles in music. The strongest cycle is the cycle of the 5th downward between roots used by Beethoven. Next, the cycle of 3rd downward between roots—used by Wagner. The cycle of the 2nd upward between roots was used by Bach.

Thru the use of cycles any imaginable combination of chords may become possible.

Write mixed cycles use only positive cycles except: the I chord may move to any chord; any chord may go to the V chord; the V chord goes to I.

Cadences:

V to I when the melody ends on the tonic note of the key is called Perfect Authentic Cadence (P.A.C.).

V to I when the melody note does not end on the tonic note of the key is called Imperfect Authentic Cadence (I.A.C.).

IV to I (C-5) is called a Plagal Cadence.

When a phrase ends on the V chord it is called a semi-cadence (half cadence).

Mixed cycles may be written spontaneously.

E.g. C2 C5 C3 C3 C5 C2 V I

Mixed cycles may also be written by the use of permutation. Permutation means getting all possible combinations of any given number of elements. Two elements=two permutations.

Exercise I: Writer mixed cycles—write basses only—in all keys major and minor.

Voice-leading (upper voices)

Clockwise	1	$\rightarrow$	3	$\rightarrow$	5	$\rightarrow$

Present chord		Next chord
1	$\rightarrow$	3
3	$\rightarrow$	5
5	$\rightarrow$	1

Counterclockwise $\leftarrow$	1	$\leftarrow$	3	$\leftarrow$	5

Present chord		Next chord
1	$\rightarrow$	5
3	$\rightarrow$	1
5	$\rightarrow$	3

C_5 and C_2	$\leftrightarrow$	= smooth
C_5 and C_2	$\leftrightarrow$	= skippy
C_3 and C_2	$\leftrightarrow$	= smooth
C_3 and C_2	$\leftrightarrow$	= skippy

Use opposite voice-leading for negative cycles.

Constant 3rd

3rd is constant in the melody. Inner may cross freely.

Write voice-leadings to all basses of last lesson:
1. Smooth

2. Skippy

3. Constant 3rd

There should never be an interval of more than an octave between any two adjacent upper voices (soprano, alto, tenor). But between the tenor and bass voices the interval may be more or less than an octave.

Symmetric Harmony

Atonal: not related to any definite key, only related to chord forms.

The 12 semi-tones of the chromatic scale are divided into equal partitions in order to form the symmetric groups. The negative cycles may be used as freely as the positive.

Symmetric harmony (chords) may be used as independent chords mixed in with diatonic chords.

Exercise I:

Write diatonic chords using 2 3 4 6 tonics mixed in.

A picture of saxophones in a window, underneath the picture, the following words: "In deciding upon the saxophone we have chosen the instrument which will serve us nobly throughout our lives forever and ever."

Dedicated to those who are kind to a fool.

Book insert (forward)

When I start the morning with a smile and do my daily duties (such as light exercise) (and health food) I am sure of the way I'm going to sound before I even blow air thru the horn. So what we have is this: an inside-the-self knowledge which brings confidence as an attribute. Or in other words by living true to those things in life which are of proven over the years value (health + exercise, good disposition, golden rule etc.), I am able to create the sound of my saxophone in my mind (at that to create the sound I want to hear) and then after "hearing" it, play it.

Book insert

When improper or more exactly when foods which are hard to digest are eaten they divert the nerve energy needed for the breathing process (playing process) and are absorbed with the task of digesting the food eaten. (REWORD)

This demonstrates how important right bodily condition is to great playing. Another case I have in mind was when I had eaten too much and in need of eliminating this food felt extremely uncomfortable when going for air (as I felt not in control of my bowels)! Yes the bowels must not be clogged and you must not be in need of going to the toilet either. As the later case proved my difficulty as I could not bring air and attack thru my horn for fear of having an accidental elimination.

Getting Our Tools

We will need tools to build our saxophone "idea." Our first tool is something to get a reflection from when we look into it. A nice still lake is a perfect looking glass. Any type of mirror is also usable. In fact a small mirror able to be carried around with you will speed along your foundation-laying. Next we want to get some books on the saxophone. There have been many and the choice here is not meant as a disavowal of the other books on saxophone which have been made available to students and/or players.

The particular 3 books which will be part of our equipment are the x, y, + z. Now we begin.

The saxophone is our friend.

He wants to make us happy. He wants to serve us. I'm glad that he's our friend (or that he likes me), because from the first moment that I saw the saxophone I fell in love with it, and wanted so badly to have one and play one. The saxophone has taught me much since that first time I laid eyes on it and it has served me well. Many times I made myself unhappy and the saxophone made me happy again. Many times I made my body sick and the saxophone made me all better again. Many, many times and forever and ever it will be so (it has promised to do so).

Also I can remember how bad and how much more unhappy I made things because of following an "un-natural" method of playing the saxophone. This volume tells of those things which seem to have been troublesome and misunderstood in this saxophonist when he was an eager beginner. Fortunately I overcame and in overcoming mistakes today I can be called an eager professional.

The use of the "air sound" which is a low, low yet possibly high tone which can be gotten through the sound of the air from the sides of the mouthpiece as the tone and crescendo is imagined (like the sound of the surf) is perhaps important beyond its correlation to the crescendo exercises of Rascher and others—being it seems suitable for generally hearing the tones in the ear before and in relation to as one constant ring; its audibility and its sensitivity, the latter referring to the hearing of the desired tone in the ear and continuing its existence with the mouth and embouchure still formed as when they were sounding: the note louder and making it audible. The note is there when heard ear-wise or sense-wise.

Also the tongue remaining on bottom (TU TA KA) until next note, exercises of Lindeman being related yet more are helped the addition of the audible breath from the sides of the mouth principle.

Use the sound of the air coming through your mouthpiece from the sides of your mouth in producing the ~ complete wave of crescendo decrescendo.

Always finish the note with the lips in same position as when last audible sound came out. Keeping the lips in this way we get softer and softer, to the end of our first wave. In other words keep the lips pursed and still in the "tone producing" position—while you bring the sound of the notes in your ear (like its echo, or reflection) slowly and gradually down to the end of the decrescendo.

The action of the playing is here emulating "exhale then retain hold contain poses and inhale retain" yoga exercise, correlating the exhale with my blow and the hold-over tone to the pause—the "hissing" along with the crescendo-decrescendo.

Saxophone and health:

The two things are "married" to each other. The very act of playing into your horn, with *increased breathing* required, brings to every saxophonist an extra measure of well-being, energy, and vitality, even though the player might not realize it. At least, *I* didn't know about this health aspect of playing until quite recently, noticing the difference in my own feeling during a period of time within which I worked and rested for two-month intervals.

There is something quite special about the saxophone. Looked down upon and shunned for so many years by the formal orchestra it has nevertheless "kept going along on its way," finding acceptance and recognition within brass ensembles and in American swing orchestras, concert brass ensembles, and within American jazz orchestras. As a matter of fact the great composers of the formal orchestra world accepted and welcomed the birth of the instrument by composing for it: Debussy + Wagner, to mention the giants.

But still the orchestra and probably the instrumentalists within the orchestra looked down and ignored the horn.

Drop the bottom jaw down as eyes are opened wide; synchronize the two oppositely pulling areas. Tongue is of course stationed, wherever, now without reading execute the above given movement.

Mongolian:

         C D E G A + C etc.

Mode on D E G A C + D etc.

Mode on E G A C D + E etc.

Mode on G A C D E + G etc.

Mode also of course on A.

So we see here that we have a scale—a Mongolian scale of 5 different tones, C, D, E, G, A, and the C above the last A which is the octave higher of the first C—which means that C, D, E, G, A, C is a 5 tone scale—many people double the C for what would be *six* notes—but alas we do not count the higher (in this case C) as a different tone.—Okay?

Modes are the same 5 tones divided into a different order of appearance, or "sequence of sounding."

On C we start our scale, C D E G A. On D we start our first mode D E G A C.

Which still as you can see contains all the tones—no more—no less—of the C scale. It is the same as the other scale—yet different and so we call it a mode of the first scale—a *mod*ification of the first scale. A *mode*. And in "natural resolution" the law is repeated for all of the notes of the C original scale—I'll complete the graph above here . . .

On the other hand, why should I have all the fun? You finish the checkerboard!

C D E G A C

D E G A C D

E

G

A

C

Now that you understand how to arrive at modes—play them. After playing them slowly and carefully, STOP.

Stop sign . . . SLOWLY and CAREFULLY—it is important that no wrong notes are hit throughout!!

Even if it takes a week before you are sure of hitting the next note correctly, wait the week. So who's in a hurry—especially to make a Boo-Boo???!!!

Now in conclusion here are some more scales—Asian 5 note scales (of differing varied origin to be sure but in order to identify them we shall use this name and keep in mind that there is no ORIGIN of *any music* in so far as geographical location of this or that music is concerned. Music sounds with their deep, warm, flowing, vibrant, "all powerful" vibrations permeating ALL SPACE + TIME in their magnificence—do they not?).

But yes, the other scales. They are first . . .

B   C   E   F   A   +   B etc.

This B scale can be treated precisely as was the C—but alas—no more today. Finish this and already you will prosper.

To maintain interest on one's own without benefit of a strict teacher, skip starting tonics at "random."

When we begin learning (or rather relearning) to breathe again we will find that just as we are ready to start measuring and controlling our respirations after having given quite enough to hear our own breaths, we are inhaling. We first exhale forcefully and then bang! We begin! We're off!

Inhaling and trying a pose or exercise or relaxation technique—
ON THE INHALE!!! Now in that particular exercise…the eyebrows are raised (which exercise incidentally stretches and massages
the eyes), while blowing into our instruments we must be sure to
BLOW and RAISE together *after* the "relax inhale."

The technique then is as follows. The first step is to look into the
mirror, focusing the upper face and eyes section of the face. The
brows do not move—nothing moves. We are trying and waiting to
get still and quiet enough to hear and count our breaths as we
INHALE~EXHALE~INHALE~EXHALE.

That's it. Now we are feeling and hearing our own breath in our
own body. It is a nice feeling. Do it as long as you desire before going
on to step #2.

In my case the first breath I take with the horn in my mouth is
an exhale—which then leads to the inhale as the action breath and
which I am suggesting is of course leading us to confusion. At least
try both ways and see if you do the same thing (or make the same
mistake). Being first conscious of the resting face while exhaling
leads to the eyebrows and movement in general (as opposed to rest)
on your first inhale!

So we now are gazing, we are resting, our eyebrows and face show
no moving. We remain like this. At rest.

1963–1973
What I Am

These uncommon men exemplified the Rosicrucian fundamental of glorifying God through serving their fellow men. Independent and in... their tho... were dedicated... ...ch for... ...de them... ...ers... ...which animated... ...lly... ...ized those who... ...tion.

...Rosicrucians to be found everywhere in... world... it is evident that the same spirit is still at work. It is evident, too, that everywhere... many... are still reaching... ...give their lives... ...be encouraged by knowing how... men of the past accomplished great things and at the same time enriched the lives of others as well as their own... ...other hope from our example and... you seek to... of others who... ...benefited by Rosicrucian instruction. This booklet may... you enlighten them and at the same time inspire you to greater accomplishment through the realization of... ...done with the... ...en prepared for... ...public distribution... ...mation may be disseminated... ...as your judgment determines.

Laziness

1. The failure to act in one's own behalf to avoid expending physical energy
2. The reluctance to act on one's own behalf for fear of expending physical energy
3. The failure to act in one's own behalf for fear of expending physical energy
4. The fear of acting in one's own behalf if it means expending physical energy
5. The reluctance to act in one's own behalf if it means expending physical energy
6. The failure to act in one's own behalf so that one can avoid expending physical energy
7. Failing to act in one's own behalf in order to avoid physical activity
8. Failing to act in one's own behalf if it entails physical activity
9. Failure to act in one's own behalf in order to avoid physical activity

The Nice time as we prepare to leave has been a substantiation of this tour. Disappointing as to the high expectations coming into it. We've gone over the reasons many times now. The problem with my horn which turned into a more serious one as I had it examined resulting in under par performances so far for all 3 concerts. We face now Toulouse where it is a possibility that we may have a decent show closer to my expectations at the start of the tour. To be fair and accurate there were some things which could be viewed as positive. More playing time for the underrehearsed group—the performance of some new material and the refining of same—the depression coming on from my personal situation leading to better understanding of same—the reminder of why the concerts must be paced as I know to do—the hearing of musical groups and meeting them which always unlocks some musical juices of my own—the decision to meet someone in Paris—the visit in Germany of a friend with a gift. All good and positive and with the benediction from my God we will be grateful, thankful, blessed, and O.T.Y.O.G. forever.

And so I was off toddling along in short rickety steps head or rather neck straightening self out head rolled freely from side to side.

And I wondered... how many children have been remanded by their elders to stop that silly way of walking and shaking yourself!! Don't be so silly boy stop it...

Each end then is a beginning.

I cannot live without Yoga. Having had my eyes opened by you, that "You" which is self-less and which is all one.

9/27/63

"Re-realized" at Festival Hall, Osaka, Japan—practicing after the concert.

#1. The organ concept can indeed be realized—as good as ever hoped for—with the holding of the low overtone indefinitely through "Scotty Breathing."² The consciousness, then, after *hearing* a *firm definite tone* immediately is able to *discern the octave* and "pick it out of the air into the instrument" so to speak. Tonight there was a very resonant dressing room which displayed no reluctance to echoing quite audible the octave. But even here the *fundamental* tone had to be of a *distinct pitch* and *clarity* before the sound which I hear "inside" under different circumstances became more *materially expressed* under the dressing-room sounding-board conditions. And so after the fundamental (conceived upon low B♭) becomes a "fixed reality" the ear of the inner consciousness must pick out the octave 5th etc. of the gamut (depending upon which are to be stressed) creating *crescendo* and *decrescendo* to the *natural rhythm of the continuously held breath* . . .

Concise sounding of the fundamental clearly—so that the octave might be *set into vibration* whereupon the gamut achieved and organ-ing be accomplished with its swells and opportunities for (double?) using stops to change not timbre.

Stopping can be used and was used in conjunction and close function with swells synchronized so as to make the "timbre change" or "stopping" more obvious and recognizable (than would it be if not used with swells must be done naturally and correctly).

Once again by "doing swells correctly" is meant the constant hearing and recognition of a clearly accurately produced Fundamental.

#2. The hitting of the complete B♭ gamut up to and including the 9th + 10th mentioned in #1 brought about the sounding of a *distinct B♭7 chord!* Striking the 9th on top (but always with a clear and distinct B♭ (either audible or within audibility) present) on some occasions or a 10th or some other partial nearby—but always maintaining and achieving the B♭7 sound by sounding the dominant and those other partials near to it—(which seem to work as a group including within it the dominant).

Thus a rediscovery of an ability now to be nurtured and developed of hitting full chords of larger dimension—when and wherever necessary or desirable!

It happened that the lights being brite caused after-images and sensations which helped by a small auditorium and backstage gave effectual visualization. A move towards one object envisioned—a turnback of apprehension and I was engaged in one movement while playing. *I dreamed with the music.*

Summary:

1. To simulate 3 + 6 (on top of a 7th chord) and being unable to jump from tonic to dominant as is the method I employ when designating a 7th chord in the bass—I can create the *same* sound of the complete full chord by putting the 7th in the bottom of my runs,

going from the 7th up to a ♭5 to the 3rd and then on to the 7th. Please memorize all semitones in the above outlined sequence.

2. Be certain to memorize all steps in the "ascending 4ths" patterns of 7th chords. To refresh your thoughts we begin (arbitrarily) at the −7 be it what it may. Now, a perfect 4th up produces the 7th to which it is related. A 4th above the dominant 7th gives *the major scale* which should be run starting on the (major) 7th or some other step, but tonic to tonic fashion. The major 7th can be used effectively for now. To continue: a 4th above this major scale produces the major 7th triad to dim triad (or just plain major) triad which begins on the dominant 7th of each and every 7th chord—providing us with much music to derive there from e.g. D-7-4→G→C major scale→F F A C E F A♭ C♭ E or E B—all G7 chord!! Memorize these exercises.

3. Keep mouthpiece and/or horn in your mouth so to fix bottom lower jaw as Rascher refers to! Practice his warm-up exercises *every* session until work time.

4. W. Tones to be done daily practicing times. 1st: ascending W.T. in major 3rds. Ascend in −3rds and watch accents. Then ascent in −3rds for 4 notes, after note 4 drop down a perfect 5th and repeat 4 note "−3 in W.T." sequence, drop down 5th after this sequence and repeat until you have culminated the cycle.

Next, to continue W.T. interest with different sounds continue with the cycle of the given first 2 bars in this exercise. Bar 1 A–C–B♭–D♭; Bar 2 B–D–C–E♭ continue on.

With this exercise we have Bar 1 A–C–B♭–D♭; Bar 2 C–E♭–F♭–F continue on.

The difference between the above being the drop in the first of a whole step between bar 1 + 2 and a drop of the half step between bars in the second exercise.

Let us now concentrate on the long-ago proven ability to sustain a line (so far the upper voice) while playing and "moving" figures below the sustained held note/line. Begin then to document the results of this ability—making pertinent notes which will formulate our laws.

8/5/63–8/11/63
During the above week at the "Showboat" a first attempt was tried and abandoned when the high pitch of the top (upper) voice "frightened me off." A later attempt however justified this first incident as the attempt proved successful to the degree that an audience reaction was noted, favorably. As to the degree attained, it was far from what is envisaged and was more or less un-controlled. Significantly enough no further attempts were made during the engagement.

10/1/63
Much un-documented progress has been achieved—confirming any and all expectations and pointing up the need for notation of advancements.

Japanese Hichiriki:

The old Egyptian double pipe which evolved to the monaulos retains the thumb hole for each hand as on the double aulos.

The instrument's Japanese descendant the Hichiriki keeps both but in practical piping the lower thumb hole is quite unnecessary and elsewhere has vanished from pipe fingering. This is why the Hichiriki has been called the most interesting woodwind living fossil.

Who knows what love is
No one seems to know
People live and people
Die, one by one
We go but just
Within this speck of
Time I found love, I know
Because of countless little things
That told me so

Opal: Milky white color, iridescent
Alabaster: White + translucent, smooth + white

The Yogi regards life as a perpetual search for meaning, an exercise in discrimination between the real and the unreal. In that spirit we shall welcome all kinds of experience both pleasant and painful and it will never harm us, for the truth lies hidden everywhere within every experience and every object of the universe. Everything that happens to us no matter how seemingly trivial throughout the day offers some tiny clue which could lead us towards wider spiritual knowledge and eventual liberation.

I am proud to be a member of the saxophone fraternity. Despite the derision with which this mystical hybrid of an instrument was initially received it has captured all! and stands today ready to lead us into the musical paths of the future!

I congratulate those being profiled and remind them to remember their illustrious brethren regularly as they journey along the path— Coleman Hawkins, Lester Young, Rudy Wiedoeft, Johnny Hodges, John Coltrane, Sigurd Rascher, Chu Berry, et al.

Intervallic Facts:
1. A perfect 4th and a major 3rd are only ? step apart.
2. From a major 3rd up or down to the dominant 7th constitutes a ♭5 interval (within a given tonic or key).
3. The −6 interval can be remembered as 3rd up to tonic (or tonic down to 3rd) of any scale.

Ending upon A♭ major, the C cluster with strong 1 and 3 partials in evidence is recommended. One way would be to run upon the A♭ major culminating at the major 7th, which would be sounded not as the single note of G but as C C and G, or as overtone #2 with 1 and 2 beneath.

Important Discovery:
Pharyngeal breathing allows for the bottom lip to be more in place
for the tone production.

On Trills Again...
On the playing of the left-hand fingers: it may be advisable to inter-
change fingers 1 and 2 in order to free the hand's upper part for
side-key trilling. So that those notes operated by finger 1 (B, Bis,...),
finger 2 must learn to manipulate as well—freeing finger 1 and the
"thumbnal area" to reach side D, E♭ etc.

Crossfingering
Since side C with the Bis depressed is more *true* (on Betsy at any
rate) we can make that stronger true C with a trill! by crossing the
right hand up to left Bis fingers and putting on B key right 3rds and
on Bis R 2. Holding this, find the side C key and depress with left
1st finger (index finger). Holding this much tone of C (strong C),
trill with right-hand thumb and finger.

Never overlook humming or imagining tone before starting.

Hum the Note
When you do (blah blah blah): HTN.
When you attempt sight reading: HTN.
When you intervalize: HTN.

When you sustain tones for "tone identification" (which when properly done assimilates the old category of "lip building" or embouchure training or what not): HTN.

Nature take me back.
I am yours.

Finality

Finality is achieved on steps 9, −3, 3, 5th, major 7th; others that can be used directly prior to final chord are +5 (V before I) ♭5, dominant 7, b9. Also the 6th had some finality to it and may be interspersed with tonic triad and major 7 if called for.

Δ on:	Produces:
9th	♭5 type finality sound
-3	Gets finality minor type sound. Also on V before I
3	Gets finality sound
4th	Not used
5th	Gets very strong finality sound
+5	Can be used with the V chord before tonic and is also effective with a minor-type ending chord

♭5	Can be used on (as with +5) a minor ending on the tonic but is hard to place at this time to a major tonic ending
6th	Can be used on V prior to I ending
Dominant 7	Can be used on V prior, or interspersed, before major ending. Some place against maybe a major 7 Δ ending (or rather before the maj 7 Δ)
Major 7	Gets ♭5 finality sound
Tonic	Not used
Flattened 9th	Used on V prior and for any abstractions calling for it on the tonic

According to Don Cherry:
Orange—E
Red—A
Blue—A♭
Green—D
Yellow—F♯
Violet—E♭

The Shakuhachi

In order to facilitate the setting of embouchure on the inhale—inhale a sound up through the instrument, which habit will keep the mouth in position.

Venus is in Virgo.

Intervallic:

Saxophone: is written an octave higher than it actually sounds.

Bass fiddle: is written an octave higher than it actually sounds.

Trumpet: is written exactly as it sounds, *as it sounds in actuality*.

Therefore whenever writing for any of these instruments: figure upon the *actual sound* as opposed to the visual appearance of the instrumented notes.

Equal division of 12 notes tones:

C E♭ E G A♭ B C

C C♯ E F G♯ A C

(A♭)

The bass would emphasize or subtly accentuate the C E and A♭.

The improvisor would then blow a chromatic run of all of the 12 tones against each and every one of the scale.

Chromatic Improvisation: Intuitive Relation of the Soloist to the Bass.

Assuming the proper intake and release of air, the other principles of Mr. Thomas are:

1. Loosening of the "back jaw muscles" without destroying the embouchure effect (lip muscles).
2. Advocating of the "unchanging embouchure" as an ideal sax technique.
3. In regard to both 1 and 2, the fact of *more* air necessary for low and for high notes was presented with the admonition that more air should not change the embouchure or tighten the back jaw muscles (which last would restrict air passage from and up thru body).
4. After establishing the sound of the tone in ear, an almost audible hum while simulating playing into the horn should be practiced—this is to effect fullness of sound and volume for these higher tones. Remember Don C's similar trumpet exercise.

   A) Also to mentally adopt a positive attitude concerning the production of these notes and to *know* that they will be hit when we go for them!! Keep to this positiveness even if an occasional miss of the desired tone occurs. This practice is related to the hum of the note and the recognition beforehand of its sound—both of which would air measurably in the "positive" approach (to be applied immediately and fast: e.g. identify then hum before hitting).

5. Imagine the notes as emanating from the bell of the horn and never, regardless of note, as from the note holes on the bore.

Questions:

What embouchure technique or exercises are good for practice?

Could some time be spent in the production of those tones above A 440 so as to visually and in actuality impress the technique of their mastery upon myself? Specifically the act of tightening the jaw muscle if demonstrated before a mirror could serve to make more vivid this point.

And please, could another explanation of the Tu, Tu, Tu, Tu principle be given?

(Too and not Tu.)

Definition of Advantages:

Things which most people who have them don't take advantage of.

MRA=Moral Re-Armament

Logical Music

We have to "release" the music.

We must be constantly alert for the sounds which will release the music.

Thurs. July, on the initial set we demonstrated the fact of this "Logical Music."

We played: "Dearly Beloved": "Dearly Beloved" was played in an improvised manner; we utilized certain effects which had been

rehearsed in sequence, in no particular sequence, but they were utilized rather, where the movement dictated.

Next we played "Oleo" and we thus concluded that set—short
—but—sweet.

The lessons to be learned are that as a group we were able to
function in a collective intuitive effort. Producing improvised music,
or rather *Logical Music.*

Format of Composition

1. All being together.

2. Throughout composition 2 instruments play together. E.g.
Sonny + Bob play together after start. Then Sonny + Bob are joined
for a dissonance by Donald which then leads to the Donald-Sonny
Duet which incidentally should suggest a different timbre than the
"dissonant 'carry over' 3 part section."

3. (Billy bears a strong resemblance to Bud Powell.) After duet
of S. + D., B. joins in for a trio which should have a Harmonic sound
rather than a dissonant sound.

4. S. + B. play duet which is followed by a sound created by B.
D. + Bob—therefore after Sonny + Billy—Billy plays shortly alone
before being joined by Don and Bob.

The sound of the 3 minus Sonny should be of a spread out timbre
with the bass on top, Don in the middle, and drums in the bass. Also
it is to be remembered that Don and Bob enter *together*, on top of
Billy.

The term *release* of the music presupposes the *fact* that the music
is in existence. We then attune ourselves by intuition and a form of

meditation into and with the music so that we become absorbed into its essence.

Closing of the eyes is a form of shutting out the objective faculties (seeing) which helps to increase the other faculties such as those necessary to produce our music.

Keep each timbre started by someone complete unto itself before changing sound. Donald was guilty of joining in with a different timbre than that which was already in progress.

Tonight, Tuesday marks an important decision—whether to send (if possible) for old horn or whether I shall find one proper setup to "sing" and carry over a group which may be antagonistic at times. I must play this horn in an open full-throated manner as the Bueschers were played, for my sound is the only one extant and must be persuasive at all times, the people having heard the trio before. Perhaps a mouthpiece can be obtained to achieve the bigness and ease of expression which is mandatory. Also the practice schedule must be attended to each day at shops or pads or at the club if necessary. After tonite's gig a great many decisions will have been reached and I trust insight into the whole horn dilemma finished.

I think I had a great nite as I did not return to this paper.

Mr. Rascher,

Ques. #1. Do you ascribe to the school which teaches breathing through the mouth—if so how does this conform to the "health breathing" dictum which instructs nose inhalation only as the nose filters with its hair the harmful qualities and poisons which float in air?

Lifting up a foot slowly while playing appropriate or descriptive music—would be playing to DRAMA!

A pre-arranged tune, a song—on the other hand—could be played (the melody and idea/meaning adhered to) and movement of a minimal nature applied to said *melodic story*.

"Ruby, My Dear."

Put then a minimal dramatic obligato to a pre-set melodic invention/son.

On "Ruby," a different movement can accompany each of the tones/notes of the initial melody, as an immediate example coming to mind.

Oh Baby, this gold, I fight to keep eyes away. Yet it is so warm, so blue, so gold...this hue...and blue, too.

'Tis true, every color is in this hue, all the landscape wears this hue.

It is the color of my skin. "Race" is synonymous to color! I am of the gold race.

My pledge:

I must bring forth my *golden light* and let it shine forth, joining the *other lights* of the firmament.

After establishing the sound and fingering of the major 3rds and/ or whole tones and/or augmenteds, you must accent each first note and think of each one as you descend in sequence.

Rule:
Whenever joining two clusters with swells for a final ending, start volume low enough that the swell may not begin until the bottom tone is produced—then swell to completion.

Since the fifth will be strong in both cases and overtone two fairly strong, the bottom fundamental must be brought forth (while hearing it) (while partials two and three are being heard) and the crescendo and definition occurring when the bottom is heard, produced, and added to the upper two partials.

Any time a 3rd involves the 4th position of the major scale (from the 6th down to it) a flat 3 will be necessary to make diatonic completion.

Drama Music
"Subtle," "unobtrusive," "minimal," "small" dramatic qualities injected into musical performing.
Subtle movement.
Drama set to music set to drama set to music set to drama set to music set to drama set to music.

Walking with a bass fiddle playing a note simultaneous with resting it down upon the floor. Stopping then for a few moments of rest and composure. Repeating then the striding for a few steps (a duration as first engaged in) and again the plucked note upon stopping and "touching down" the instrument to the floor. Again a pause for reflection, for rest, to regain composure, and we lift up our fiddle again and stride forward—continuing in this manner until the stage position or playing position is reached or, when not entering, until action requires.

Today, hear for the first time, the theoretical designation of B♯ and the aesthetic realization of it join and yoke as the inner mental hearing of F♯ rejects it as a major 7 of the preceding F♯. Not so with the thinking of E♯!!

Whether or not the tone is sounded the sequence or cycle is carried through to its completion. The air flow must still proceed into the horn at the same (or as close to as possible) rate of release being kept up, steady, just as if the note were being heard to its conclusion— when the stomach has emptied its air smoothly, rhythmically, and flowingly steady into the horn.

Check on composer (maybe French??) name: Cameron.
    Similar to medley of songs done on Japanese tour (by myself)

85

and with only strains of songs done in rapid succession in different keys.

"To send forth light into the depths of the human heart"—the Artist's Task.[3]

And a reasonable one. For within each human heart, or the heart of every human being, there waits patiently an abiding spirit, which finds expression and recognition at the hearing of a true musical rendering... by the artist.

Don't go beyond where you get a bang out of playing. Each day is different.

Always derive the natural fun and pleasure which is part of every saxophonist's birth-right.

The tongue stays limp until the attack is started.

For some time now I have enjoyed the reputation of being modest where my own achievements are concerned. In fact, I have on several occasions been admonished by my friends and colleagues for being too humble about my work, and not appreciative of my own talent. Finally, on at least a few occasions I have been accused of being insincere, and in this, not being modest at all. This last I ignored. The opinion of my friends, I considered.

Try to recall the following:
Crescent—John Coltrane
Horace Silver with Woody and Joe if possible
Ornette Coleman, *At the Golden Circle*
Some "mournful" solo Scottish piper playing

The remembrance of the sound and tune played by the single Scottish piper for the three (?) girls to dance to inspired this figure.

Fastly articulated As on FAC, FAC, FAC etc. Then do the same thing starting on E and repeated E G♯ B, E G♯ B etc.
    Produces a strong *Flamenco* feeling.

The new Selmer seems to like and respond to G concert, and we can dream.

What does Lester play on "Dickie's Dream" and "Countless Blues"? Sax or clarinet?

All time, rhythm, and harmony are pulsating, sounding, resounding, and happening according to the grand symphony which is constantly being played.

All sounds, when discerned in this context, are rhythmically and harmonically involved and fit.

There is a B concert blast from a foghorn, car horn, or whatever heard often in the London streets.

It would be the length of a foghorn blast, and was heard repeated two or three times.

Its equivalent for my horn is either C♯ on the staff of a lusty, "round toned" C♮. If it is the latter it must not be a thin note.

Here again we use the tongue to help us intone properly by keeping it away from the reed—plus alternating it from mouth roof to floor according to the difficult notes involved.

Plus: don't forget that the ultimate, as now conceived, would have all notes played by the tongue behind mouthpiece, either on roof or floor but out of the way of the reed. Therefore there are no fixed rules on tongue position—as it will eventuate in the tongue being in a *neutral* spot until called upon *positively*.

The fact that the taste is seen to be so much more beautiful when returning after an imposed restraint...

What does it mean?

A) That it is a reward for abstaining. (That would be a perversion of a thought.)

B) That the lesson to employ is moderation (but *indulgence*...).

C) Beware please of the guiles of a costumed lady! So that all that I am doing in actuality is devising mental means of convincing myself that the truth is not the truth, does not exist, and should not be listened to. Don't hear the voice!

I hear this. Let's begin stopping now, Sonny. Okay? The date is today.

Don't worry about the race, worry about the pace.

Holding tone to climax point—having control of the breath must be realized.

What I am is jazz phrasing. This thing which jazz is all about, which they are all still trying to do.

I am also jazz timing.

Always use tone imagination. A mental hearing of sound desired.

Uniformity of character and volume on every note.

Do not forget, and do remember, to end notes with the CAA, CAAA, CAAAA not with the tongue joined up to the reed—as for so long mistakenly done!!!

He must possess adaptability, courage, tolerance, generosity, patience, perseverance, and sincerity.

Even the fish must go.

The designations which exist in scale B are identical to those which are used by myself. I related W.T. scales to major scales so that each member of a W.T. scale is as well the name of a major scale and/or key note.

Thus scale B has indeed Db, Eb, F, G, A, B, all major scales key notes and name tones in it.

Instead of scale As G♯ + A♯ which are not within the major scale name gamut, we use Ab + Bb which are as well "major tone starting scale names," giving us then for scale A the notes Bb C D E F♯ Ab. The practicality of such a synthesis can be readily seen, as we practice and associate rather than practice without association.

But we think of the Eb which is an octave below while we produce + finger the Eb shown. Contrary notion determines the octave which is used, so that if (as we have shown) A is followed by the note in an ascending sequence, the thought-of and "heard" octave would be of an ascending direction.

If as in bar 2 the 2nd tone is descending the reverse is true.

Remember please the importance of keeping the fingers over the keys during these exercises in particular so that Eb in bar one is positioned by fingers before sounding.

Rebirth of Hindu Music: pages to record

Page 20, 2nd para. which gives credence to my new or now resolved way of playing—even to the admonition of wrong notes.

Our music must revitalize + energize our fellow men. Invest them with ambition where lethargy resides. Give them courage where failure has borne fear. (Hig. + Cherry, e.g.)

Page 27 on to page 28 (especially para. 2 and para. 3).

"Tone & Soul are One," if tone + soul are not one then we have no *real* tones, but mere "notes." Sonorous shells. (page 29)

Page 30 para. 2 condemning or evaluating European formalism nicely. Going on in this criticism to page 31 and on to pg. 34 where the following stands out from para. 2:

"We hear MUSIC with our ears

We read MUSIC with our eyes

We experience MUSIC with our heart,

Thus we have sensorial, intellectual, and spiritual music."

Page 35 again sums up the task involved in precise manner.

It's not the race,
It's the pace!
So run it with Taste
More than with Haste

My forte and hopefully the essence of jazz is creative improvisation which attribute, by the way, makes it (jazz) more alive, vital, and "god like" (creative aspect) than any other music form can possibly be. This is not meant as a declaration of a dominance of jazz as a form of music over so called classical—for Beethoven, Bach, and the men whose music still lives today all created and improvised just as the creative jazz musician of today does. To create—on the spot—intelligently—intuitively—and with feeling and emotion: this then is man in his finest hour—portraying nature.

While attending to shaving and massage pressing the face, the strain and tire (felt before) of the upper arms (along the inside if standing hands at sides palms out) and above the elbow ([it now seems at least] more than the lower area below) was noted and later the concentrated "thought pressure" to the same area facilitated a more seemingly natural normal standing position. The arms then by being attended to mentally are furthermore held and kept back away from body more which posture when assumed immediately and/or automatically exercised the back of the neck spinal area—which as Mr. Oki pointed out is a very important body region for me.

11/1/64 Chicago

Nov. 11, 1964
As far as my career goes I have no doubt that my continuazation is assured and inevitable.

My knowledge or rather ability far supersedes the normal and/or average in my field.

Furthermore, all "steady" periods of work sharpen (and make more ready to present physically) this ability.

Each succeeding period now seen to be just that!! When further the deceleration can be seen to affect by shortening the inactive periods between cycles, the great power which must be mirrored in kindness to others is magnanimous indeed.

Dear Mr. Oki,

Just now it is the 25th day of February and plans for the Yoga group are coming along much better than one should hope for. Especially one who has been so uneven in his daily postures and Asanas!! And yet even as I try to shake sadness and gloom about the events of the past few months, it becomes impossible to do so. Rather than relate to you my disappointment with myself I shall simply say thanks to the ALMIGHTY and to my mortal teacher and guru—

"Mr. Oki."

I can now do the lotus pose fairly well, even though I have missed practice often.

I begin with right foot on left thigh.

Rule

All of the personal appearances must be previewed in terms of what are the physical properties of the establishments. This is because we must always begin the sets away from the bandstand. After finding our key/mode/groove, through a series of statements we gradually involve ourselves with the rhythm and the sound and make our way to the bandstand in a rhythmic manner. Almost a dance! For after all do we not do everything in rhythm?

Don may blow his horn by having it available between sets (depending on layout of engagement) or may blow mouthpiece—which could be kept available during intermissions. Billy could—naturally—beat on anything available on the way to the drums. Bob will simply make his way to the bandstand immediately and join in at a propitious moment. This will also soften the effect of everyone coming to the stand and making adjustments as Bob can lead on certain passages to emphasize the stage with him on it at any time when a lag develops for any reason, besides the above-mentioned physical adjustment reason.

All should have watches set to the minute at the beginning of every night.

The start of a set will be on a signal of an exact moment—this way we will all be ready to answer each other if the situation so necessitates—which at the beginnings it will call for this conversation to find the mode which we all hear.

Uniform Embouchure

Keep bottom lip in a "firm" position on such tones as B, C, C♯, D, D♯, E, F, F♯ (G + A♭) when attempting to produce them perfectly and properly.

This "firmness" is of course to be *constant* which it seems to be in most other registers—even *above* the A♭ mentioned!

Chest remains raised.

94

Attempt to simulate the embouchure position used on "lower tones" for the higher tones as well.

If an extended jaw occurs easily and naturally when producing e.g. low F, the *identical* jaw and embouchure position must be used in following that low F with for example a high F (above treble).

This is what *actually* occurs and is consequently more than an abstract situation used for example.

Chest remains raised.

The change from D♭ to B when descending W.T.-wise is enharmonic and requires for this and other reasons a more conscious focus while executing them.

G to F however also enharmonic presents no such difficulty which points to the D♭ key (meaning key as scale) and the B key as being more to account for the slowing down of thought during their sequence.

A♭ to F♯ also being enharmonic causes the same concern, especially as in "exercise Maupin" where we must have A♭ to be immediately followed by A♯ (descending W.T. triads).

I would like to see the film "alone" with my instrument before bringing in the group for a rehearsal-showing. This would establish tonality of the sketches—still, the overall sound of the group would possibly change the tonality once again. I cancel then the suggestion. After a minimum of rehearsal (1 or 2 days) of my score outlines by group—a complete session should be had with group + film showing. Arrange then outline sketches on the suggested music—e.g. a sketch or more on (cheerful music), a sketch or several if necessary upon (cheerful "Alfie's Theme"), a sketch and outline on "Lily

Pastoral" theme. Something, anything—just enough to have a part for everyone (if necessary) on each of the suggested themes. Not until after seeing and hearing the band and picture at the first rehearsal showing am I really decided upon an appropriate theme. The elementary (or the sketch) themes serve here to establish a working attribute among the band and also to have a "starting point" at the time of the first multi-showing where the director and others shall be aboard. Their criticism of that first sketch music will allow me to act accordingly with the next phase, which will be the "*brand new*" compositional theme necessary for the result—and which should be able to be played with the film not more than a day or so later when more attention can be placed on the timing of music parts by myself as the project comes of age and is ready to be "final cut."

1. Pencils sharpened.
2. Call L.G. concerning his idea of what theme should be (or be like) for this Friday evening (Oct. 22, 1965).
3. A fast ¾ of the "fast theme" as part of the rehearsal of band and as a variation of this theme which can be actually done a thousand different rhythms and tempi. This would also enlarge the emotional spectrum of the band.

Tuesday
Take Bueschers to 46th St. Get the hell out of New York. Explain to Dr. N. my predicament. Begin zeroing in on first rehearsal date. Watch diet today.

Friday 5/25

All of the above have been done—the diet alone needs to be curtailed. Time is short. The mouthpiece practice is quite effective.

Sat:

Mouthpiece practice

Some listening

Diet (restrict quantities)

3 cups of coffee—4 hamburger rolls/butter

This upon awakening.

Now 3 packs of bitter lemon candy which has now informed me
    that my stomach reacts to the sweet adversely therein.

Still Saturday:

And what a revealing thing. The sweets immediately caused stomach
    cramps and the inability to breathe with stomach.

Just dig that again.

THE INABILITY TO BREATHE WITH STOMACH.

Breathing is the necessary part of playing my instrument. Please
    refrain from eating these in the future.

Rest of Saturday:

Some listening.

Watch diet again.

Diet still uncontrollable.

But am fighting!?!

More music please.

I am a *singular* artist.

I do a singular thing.

Philosophy point A.

"The only thing worth doing is nothing."

Philosophical counter B.

"Only the 'peace' of 'nothing' can be attained through only action."

Dear Friends,

"The practical application" after knowledge comes.

The lemon must be fully appreciated as the provider of lemon oil and rubbed, gripped, shaped, pressed lightly as well by the hands before assimilation.

Note:

The coda (which forms a neat "ramp" repetition-interlude) may be played on and extended upon, always however ending with a final 8 of the original strain. *Moment* and *mood* will of course always dictate any variations and one must therefore be *open* and *flexible* for such changes whenever they occur.

Thank you.

You may use the chords from the bridge at the 1st 8 during improvising choruses for, while doing so, you are enveloping and putting into a passage, so to speak, the sound—the complete sound color given off—tone—mode—feeling...

Thus everything has its own sound. Every song has its sound or predominant "tonal ringing" left in your ears. The suggestion then is that this *law* validates any such conduct that is indicated above.

This is no laughing matter.

Since it is hereby revealed:

This most lowly one pledges to close the current pattern with perhaps and at the very most *please Sonny*—a small panic insurance discretely escorted to the Ronnie Scott scene and engagement at which time turn-ons will still be outlawed remembering again that panic can never be accomplished on such a bountiful scene and shouldn't therefore be *outlawed* (or rather) tolerated and the thought even entertained. Finish Mr. P directly and keep to the resolve—this the very night of Wednesday, March 9, 1966.

The importance of the now experienced breakthrough in the body consciousness and conditioning (what with the nose and lower back to toes "exercises") renders it out.

Now to bathe and wash socks and be clean for the big day tomorrow to fix up horn at Ponte's and to be on the NEW RESOLVE 100% from the time done (before sunrise probably) till England.

As I might have guessed the resolve was broken but only after a longer than before period of abstinence was maintained. So now continue—!

Before you go to sleep at nite
and when the day is through

please bring to mind the day's events
to pass them in review
the things I planned to bring about
that didn't quite come true
one by one by one by one
the tasks begun, then left undone

a) No more food today.
b) Mike set up sound system for V.V. instead of synthesizer or Moog.
c) Musical identity crisis of tonal concept—tone production (mine) as the basis of my music—as opposed to sounds induced from Moog.

All of the above as related to the Vanguard and my own feeling of getting used to a brand-new mouthpiece/teeth/teeth/mouthpiece accommodation and the fact that I need maybe a different backup (as we have discussed).

Masuo's playing behind me I find extremely inappropriate especially for my own *creative mechanism*. I may be able to use a McBee, a Haden, at this point. I'm at the Vanguard. I have to be honest. I have to experiment towards finding *my* sound. Yes or no?

Now in so doing I am facing upcoming club dates immediately following. You've got to be up for the Vanguard—yes.

You also have to be up for a road night club in a different way —yes.

In a way more like I did Europe, in that band's way.

So how do you compare and prepare for an entirely new bunch

of beans—needing presumably the rehearsal and work from the one gig to prepare for the latter?

d) How would you like to play the Moog in the group? You can just start out adjusting the patches for the horn and then add a note here and there, a sound here and there, etc., ???

e) My idols were guys like Percy France and John Hill.

f) I am happy for a "select group who have heard Sonny" (*really heard him go*) because a larger group means more meddling by them in my affairs.

g) I may even be able to use Don Pate. But to do so involved my being miked above the fender. Which is fine. I also need some private moments—more perhaps unmiked Rollins—personal Rollins—intimate etc. If so the difference in the trio sound levels would cancel each other out.

h) There are more esoteric sides to my playing and they need to be fed right now with a new background/backup. Where I can experiment more with phrasing and fashioning my own thing.

i) On the other hand the reproduction of sound now becomes a big hassle. Example: Dr. Nelson: "Don't put too much strain on those teeth; don't rest the horn on teeth."

The above being considered, consider that the thing needs a bed for it to rest on to get anywhere near into it.

j) The next concert I do should involve something unique and applicable as a point of interest. E.g. special work by someone for me, what have you.

The Vanguard Monk engagement now in its final week has found me recouping some earlier lost audiences these past few nights (about from the latter part of the week #2). Whenever I start walking into the audience it is a sign of closer relations as well as proving a valuable tool of performance which I feel I must earn before I start doing it. Tonight I am beat and must nonetheless continue in the upswinging vein.

A great musician must be a man of great spiritual status—ascetics and yogis or disciples of great saints.

Music is a *divine* revelation.

Pythagoras and Gautama: contemporaries

	Color	Nervous reaction	Perfume
C	Red	Stimulates but quickly fatigues	Camphor, geranium, sandalwood
D	Orange	Stimulates with tonic effect, cheerful and forceful	Vanilla, clematis, heliotrope, almond
E	Yellow	Activity, clear thinking	Jasmine, cassia, citrus, iris

F	Green	Balance, relax-ation, + harmony	Musk, benzoin, narcissus
G	Blue	Healing and soothing	Syringe, lilac, frangipani, sweet pea
A	Indigo	Inspiration and self-control	New hay, lavender, balsam
B	Violet	Peace + calm, higher-plane healing	Carnation, menthol, peppermint, cinnamon

Everything is good.
Natural truth.
Habit—exercise.

1) Maintain the smile with teeth parted.
2) Move tongue from roof to bottom with no movement of rest of face (particularly bottom teeth will tend to move upwards). Keep this up.
3) While so doing gain concentration at level of eyes.
4) While maintaining all of the above directions...look into the eyes and allow them to emphasize and do the good work of the excrcise.
5) Which is done by allowing the smile to fade as the concentration goes to the tongue—feeling for its native nerves as it slowly

moves the tongue from mouth's roof to mouth's bottom all the while the face fading gradually as it does naturally. Continue to face fade . . . returning to a relaxed pose as it fades in rhythm to the tongue's realization and all this happening *without the teeth moving*. Only the face's contours relax around (so to speak) the stationary teeth in which moves the tongue up + down, up + down.

Alternate between upper center flesh (as described below) and lower center flesh (as described below) at an even rate and in rhythm naturally. There comes an actuation of tonsil area where this strain is felt. Remaining momentarily on one pose will relieve strain felt upon which one may continue to alternate poses again.

Tongue in pose A + B feeling as a guide and with the tongue that part of the gum where the division or center flesh exists above the top center teeth and between the lower mandible center teeth.

This is an attempt to document certain exercises which came to me at various times. Once this diagram has been looked at, however, the possibilities away and beyond what is here shown will no doubt present themselves to which you should partake of the invitation and improvise at will.

P.S. The connecting center "flesh center" must not be feared when felt and if you begin to massage it too vigorously while going for same you may feel instead on the upper right side of the teeth instead of feeling the center.

There seems to be a lack of control of the sinus area, an inability to control the nerves and muscles. It seems furthermore that by not biting and chewing squarely on both sides of the mouth this condition has come to be. There is for certain a relationship of the above with the swallowing "sense" (consciousness).

[Dr. Nelson, is it true that lost teeth result in sagging facial muscles due to the idle areas or pockets (connected between teeth + nerve) thusly brought about?]

Biting or rather chewing on both sides of the mouth would I am presuming waken or reawaken the sinus passage area with its relative throat and swallowing connections. At the current time it appears the "front tooth" is in some way preventing (thru its sensitivity) the proper masticating of the left-side back teeth. Exactly what effect would the removal of this tooth have upon my ability to chew on both sides and then also on the stability of the orthodontic bridge in remaining seated properly?

It would appear then that this tooth seems to be too long and that if it could even be shortened there would be less of a sensitivity when it meets the upper teeth.

Dr. Nelson: You once said (I think) that teeth should not be clenched but teeth slightly apart. I assume this is intended to alleviate wear on bridge work.

I have been paralyzed on my face in these areas and am now regaining their health.

In order to work and exercise the atrophied nerves and muscles of the face the clenched teeth seem to be necessary. At least for the time being until a nerve consciousness and/or realization is experienced in this area.

Dr. Nelson—may I look at my X-rays again and would you explain the shadows in all their implications to me.

Don't view things as natural I want to possess.

Now, a second later the ring around the moon has changed to a more scanty view of the "lunarsphere," now completely gone from sight—"voilà" as in a magic trick. Earlier when I first came into the fairgrounds it was "standing there" beaming down upon everyone, big, full, and almost overlooked, seeming to be one of the huge massive beautiful modern orbital exhibits itself. Its color? I'll take a crack at it . . . a "burnt yellow." It seemed although subtle toned to be as well glistening and shimmering—reminding one of gold.

The B♭ occurring (for tenor) directly below my B (alto) was sung and *rung*, it subsequently being analyzed as a tonal sound which "bell-like" quality has previously escaped me. Therefore the directive of this 23 day of August 1964 A.D., to attain (through possibly held sustained resonating tones [for one method]) this bell-like ring on my BB (A♭ concert) directly under my B. Thanking you Oh God I remain your faithful student.

Analysis of an Attitude on "Sometimes I Summer Like a Motherless Time"

If on the contrary we conceive a fifth as a pleroma instead of as an interval we deal with a portion of musical space which is a fullness of tone, with a host of tones theoretically infinite in number, no longer with two abstract notes with emptiness in between, but with a pleroma of compact, homogeneous sound-substance.

In acting upon our realization of the effects of tobacco on the human body, Prophet and myself found a contentment and happiness far more enjoyable and satisfying than that particular feeling of temporary sensory exhilaration which results from the inhalation into the lungs of cigarette smoke.

Once we intellectually reasoned out the physical or bodily reaction to the introduction of tobacco fumes, we could not feel *justified* in continuing its use.

The constant reference to "willpower," then, is misleading. There must be rather a conclusion reached as to the merit of a particular thing—a judgment constituting what can be called and what has been often referred to as RIGHT + WRONG.

Once a human being so decides it is a simple fact of nature that health and happiness results from acting according to your own decisions and pain, sickness, disease, and unhappiness results from rejecting your own understanding and decision.

Once such a judgment has been made by an individual he is for the rest of his life bound by it. Therefore when one acts according to *his own* (not someone else's) reasoning, health, happiness, and satisfaction result + when one disregards and rejects *his own* (not someone else's) reasoning, pain, disease, and unhappiness are the result.

It is this simple, natural, proper, + easily understood fact of nature which should be looked to as the answer to habitual uses of undesirable substances and not "willpower."

Childish—that's childish, this is childish—he acted too childish.

But wouldn't a better word be "egotistical"?

He acted so egotistical—that's egotistical, or what have you.

The reason we use the term is because we recall being and acting this way during an age when we were around our loved ones. Our loved ones expressed their love by making us wrap up before we went to the store in the rain, by making us put rubbers on etc. etc. We as human beings (of any chronological age of development, it doesn't matter) need to be *loved*—to know that someone loves us— *really*—enough to hurt our feelings (*sic* ego) when such is necessary for our own safety and protection.

The love is measured by the degree of resistance we show.

This is another case of the human heart searching for love.

A natural condition is sought by that heart—a normal condition.

Stand erect, feet together, hands along sides. Inhale deeply while raising your arms (keeping the elbow straight) high above your head until your palms join each other.

Even as we learn scales and "run" sound patterns on scales, we must prepare for the time when we forget these same scales and patterns—turning them instead into thoughts expressed, rather than as musical equations recalled, so that when we actually go out to play and start improvising we may stop unconsciously remembering and thinking and studying and recalling and allow the music which is as we have pointed out already in the air just waiting for us to relax and let it come out of us and our horns.

Music is in the Air.

Music of the American Indian

It is less for entertainment and more used for + associated with RELIGIOUS, CEREMONIAL healing, and other of the "higher activities." Indeed there is or has been a strong magical suggestion about the Indian's musical practices, and these are closely bound up with his PANTHEISTIC creed. In general, songs are looked upon as INSPIRATIONS not as CREATIONS—and there is nothing corresponding to the "popular song" of the European races. A marked mannerism of singers is attacking the note on its sharp side and then settling to its proper pitch, an excessive tremolo, and a detachment note from note by a curious contraction of the GLOTTIS.

It is mostly all UNISON, with generally a pentatonic scale.

Eliminating bothersome ledger lines and placing the horn in its proper pitch relationship with its pianoforte reading as well as encouraging the use and mastery of what is a "perfect" range—for both playing and writing.

C D E♭ F G A B♭ C
Sir and Brother Isaac Newton's corollary to the color spectrum is also an authentic Dorian mode.

From Nature the saxophone gets its shape, as did the first horns played by early man—(animal horn, the curvature).

From Ancient Egypt it borrows its "flute" form and from the trumpet-type instruments from modern metallurgy it brings its brass metal. From the woodwinds and from the wood from nature's garden it gets its reed.

It is yesterday, today, and tomorrow all in one form—the almighty saxophone.

Experiences while open-air practicing have been many and numerous. One case comes to mind. It seemed that I suddenly found myself really "vibrating" musically, sounds and tones and rhythms, and I was falling right into ideas and perfectly executed sequences and into divine modulations. And I would then get responses by the birds who are really quite good musicians and willing and anxious to join your orchestra as well!!!

And so I knew then that—

Tasmanian Tiger:
Pouched domesticated dog, similar to greyhound.

Different Ways to Play

1. With tongue at mouth floor, bottom lip covering bottom teeth, top teeth biting and to take a breath open up—leaving bottom embouchure still more or less in position.

   Alas!

   The top teeth biting and then to breathe open up—you see is incorrect as the top teeth and muscles of upper face do not, cannot, and will not move. It is the *lower* which only *moves*!

2. A) The teeth biting on top and remaining this way, even and while the breathing process of "bottom lip—jaw dropping" is in process (or in operation). Tongue on roof of mouth during breathing and blowing.

   B) The same as A) except for the tongue position which is here placed upon the mouth's floor during all playing, breathing, + blowing.

   C) When playing, special care must be given to the various bodily parts which are affected and "touched" by the breath as it travels thru the body and into the instrument (see Hindu Indian Music volume, section on "throat teeth" singing).

3. The same as #2 except for again the tongue's placement—which is here held against the inside of the lower lip and the outside of the lower front teeth—throughout all playing.

David—please cannot you play *one note in vamp style* until you know just what I'm playing, and then if it is something we have played (and/or change from vamp) would be directed by me at the proper moment.

3 pants
1 suit
—pressed
3 shirts
2 jackets
—clean

"Artificial Heart Lung Machine"
Mitral valve (?)
Pulmonary valve
Silicone rubber stainless steel Teflon
Upper heart chamber
Veins
Arteries

To Read:
The Radio Engineering Handbook, Keith Henney

Sit-ups to reduce and slim waistline:
Lie flat on your back with arms outstretched behind your head. Now sit up and touch toes. Then return to starting position and repeat. (It may be necessary to put feet under heavy object.)

Sativa must be curtailed now notice head-stomach disarrangement. This is another perfect time for a perfect act, as with the diet/fast.

Tonite rinse mouth with salt water. Do washing (gloves). Call Lucille. Dig how c. resin makes you do less and feel more tired. I think I would be better off if I just worked throughout each day—I would have more energy.

It was a marvellous evening. Yesterday has been a little humid but then the breezes had started and today the fresh air vacuumed everything out. The grass and trees and bushes were so green and clear. It's supposed to go to 45 tonite. I've been eating fruit and broiled chicken for my diet while I'm up here in the country. So far one big meal a day. For instance I had today two mangoes, half a broiled chicken, two small cantaloupe, plus my juice which I drink throughout the day. Grape, pineapple, papaya etc. I want to write much more now. I want everyone to know just what I go through.

I had to put some spit in my horn.

Tell Miles he's my leader.

Treatise: why I stopped relating to standards.
    This is a certain time in which I am trying to project a certain image of myself so I just wanted to be sure about what you had in mind.

Ask Mingus if there is anything he wants me to play for him at Newport.

Show Lucille again how I fucked up my own nose making it more bulbous. A way of hurting myself because of my guilt feeling re: my musical inefficiencies.

As I look in mirror—too much fat ass. I must fast and/or regulate today but it just seems to be such a good time for fasting. As stomach is sick. This is what you can call "a message to Garcia."

Definitely too much fat around behind. Cool it.

Before last weekend:
Buy new ECM 50
Call Charles Mingus
Pray to God.

When I get high, I get closer to God.

Ask Charles: is it about eating and putting a roof over your head? Is that what life amounts to?

Or "Is that *all* life is about," correctly put.

Fast today and/or regulate.

Leg raises to reduce the lower abdomen:
Lie flat on your back with arms outstretched behind your head. Now raise your legs to a 90 degree angle then lower them slowly back to starting position. You may need to hold on to something heavy at first.

I'm old, I'm tired. My friends are trying to tell me to give up. I feel like giving up.

All of the business part is devoid of moral underpinning. It enables me to function but lessens my moral fiber— my commitment, purpose—in other words, the only commitment I have now is to getting food for my next meal. Of course when I perform I endeavor to do what I seem to have to do and try to get into a trance-like state as seems to be what allows me to do this thing for which I am being paid and for which the bread for tomorrow's meal comes.

The point about the Gita's view of work is that if I deteriorate or am not up to snuff I should not expect success and should gracefully exit. But I cannot participate with a priori view of negativism. I have to keep practicing and hope that I can improve a little musically but basically by practicing derive the mortal underpinning to keep it happening, and to keep trying to make it happen.

Look on procrastination as a good thing. It is an act which admits to the realization (Hindu) of the inevitable occurrences of life (blood, pain, seemingly negative occurrences) without a view of keeping the lid on an existing situation. I have at times wanted and wished for time to stand still at a particular certain moment. If it would all stay this way this would be heaven. But of course (reality) the other side of the whole soon reappears. Things are never constant. Disaster is coming. Disasters are coming.

I like to play and let the crowd settle and then lull and then wake them up with something *outrageous*. This is from playing and digging the crowd (which diminishes what you play) so that just when they begin to lose interest I shock them back to reality (start thinking music rather than observing crowd) the reality of me, me and my sound, my communication through ancient ritual sound.

Explain to Lu how we are fighting THE SYSTEM in this Boston thing (as in everything else).

It's all about that people want to control you/present you/picture you as they want you to be/fit *you* into *their* category. This constitutes what life out here is all about; the battle lines, as it were. This is where the system tries to crush *us* as it did *me* one time. Watch yourself.

They try to blackball you in the business, to bring you in line. I'm working on this album and we gonna tell 'em *F 'em*.

The goal of the ruling interests (corporate) is to keep this society and the entire world open for maximum profitability regardless of the human or environmental costs.

Inside of me
Songs of mystery
And then I see Nubia

1979–2010
Legacy

Book titles:

Breaking Down the Jazz Wall: Minorities Within Minorities, by Sonny Rollins

Bridging the Gap Between Mental and Physical, Including Theory of Loop Imagery, by Sonny Rollins

Lord—use my troubles to bring beautiful harmony to my life.
Lord—shine your light on every problem I have and show me its beauty.

Oct. 22, 1979
Beginning of journal of "ESP" feelings, SR/LR communication.
1) LR had strong sense that she had "taken over" SR illness—confirmed later. SR ate some "bad" fish & expected to be sick (in Bellingham, Wash., or Eugene, Oregon). Instead LR got *very* sick Monday night, so sick that she was unable to go to city for appts on Tues. (no apparent cause). She had the feeling (confirmed 3 days later) SR had not gotten sick & this was *his* illness.

Oct. 24

2) LR had strong feeling that this day was the "beginning of her death." She planned to buy a notebook or diary & record what happened.

Later, in the early AM of the 25th, SR suggested, before knowing of the death thoughts, that LR record other things.
Early AM 25th—SR NYC, LR Germ.
3) LR asleep, had dream in which her mother was alive & lying down (as she was at time of death) & mother & LR holding conversation. First dream of mother since latter's death Sept. 28.

In same *dream* phone rang & when LR picked it up, no one there.

Right after that (almost 3 AM)—SR called—unexpectedly—since we had talked ~12:30 AM—he had feeling he should call.

Suspenders:
34 inches long from back snap to front snap

Favorites:
"I'm Gonna Sit Right Down and Write Myself a Letter," Fats Waller
"The Man I Love," Coleman Hawkins
"Lover Man," Billie
"Beautiful Moons Ago," King Cole Trio
"Another Hair Do," Charlie Parker
"Afternoon of a Basie-ite," Lester Young

By weight:

If you were at 182

Being at 182 for instance does not mean the same depending upon the shrinkage factor presently existing in the body.

There is a way of just being at 182 but with the cells being fatter and more open to fat intake so that you will tend to go in the upper direction from 182.

Then you can be at 182 but have your cells more empty so that they will just maintain 182 but will tend to go in the downward direction from 182.

By making your circles + think massage of area + proper positioning of the area you are exercising.

Look in the mirror, tighten the area—as you would want it to look—integrate this tightening with a circle and make your circles. Important—tighten all other bodily muscles before, if possible.

I can only listen to the Crusaders a little at a time. At least with the Stones the free spirit is more implied if not there. I understand the immediacy of slickness however at a certain point it offends. Of course I am seeking a middle road on all these matters. At least for records which should be a little more contrived.

Generate certain frequencies which can bring animals under your sway.

As a wind player you have the possibility of all frequencies such as dog range and all animal ranges.

Jack:
This is for the sake of the music I'm saying. I don't want to stop you from doing your thing. And I don't want you to stop me from doing mine for the sake of the music.

Since I don't control any aspect of music but my own self-expression I would like to play some in order to realize my own potential. Through salvation we can hopefully reach our own spiritual salvation. In other words I don't care about the ego thing—as long as I can feel musically fulfilled. Do you hear what I'm saying?

As far as the set was concerned there is no doubt of the musical level of it; it was high. And I appreciate that. And I appreciate your doing it.

It's time for me to begin making cosmic music. It has nothing to do with EGO.

You see, since how I look is [...] extremely to most whites (my erstwhile fans), and since I cannot basically change my look (I must wear a beard due to jawbone loss) means being my natural grey. This is something which is very important to me.

It happens all the time, I know—but it's not going to happen to me. You guys have forgotten that you are here to play for me. You're supposed to be playing *for me*. Accompanying me! Helping me to do something. If along the way you can score points for yourself as individuals, fine. But when you start as you guys are now doing—not playing for me . . .

You see . . .

I have the impression that you guys are not playing for me anymore. And I can't deal with it.

Ask me to explain the "Wheel of Life" as exemplified by the "Hindu" poster I saw in India.

By being out to improve *you* alone. This is what borned the Me Generation.

This is *my* answer to what I find here in the world, isn't it.

Assuming that I was one of the fathers of the me generation —my idea was to not be only after perfect body—but mind, self-consciousness, & understanding.

BAND
Build 2nd ½ of *Don't Ask*.

Don't get soft in there.

Play "Boys" with that suspension vamp on pushing B♭7 into top of "Harlem Boys."

When checking out tenor at Pineus check left-hand D side feeling—it must be fat! Also the following E♭ E F F♯ G A♭ A B♭ B C C♯ D E♭ E F etc. (although I seem to remember that as being trickier).

Approach band on new theme of duos trios explain that I will have
   to be on stage.
Lu—I want critics to knock me so that I come back and make them
   look like fools. This forms part of my motivation.
Al's playing too much on 1 level acoustically which prevents me from
   creating.
I am now playing a Ponte reed which is in horn packet.

Despite his prodigious talent I was always loath to place M.A. in
that sacrosanct category occupied by Joe Louis + Ray Robinson his
immediate predecessors and my boyhood heroes. Still, my reserva-
tions aside, he was unquestionably one of the game's most colorful
champions.

   However there are things in life which I daresay transcend others.
In the case of M.A. his courage on moralistic grounds in confronting
the most powerful nation in the world has certainly made him one
of the most important figures of the 20th century, a man beloved
by Americans of all ethnic groups and races, across the board.

   I wonder though how many people as I do feel somehow deflated
watching him these days doing T.V. commercials?

21.8.1981
As long as I am alive,
I feel certain to overcome everything, always.

Health has been bad recently. Leg, feet, mouth, body weight, eyes.
Also cut knee.
This is April of 1982.
July of 82.
Mental depression—physical draining.

Remember Japan's going to be about shape and fitness and clothes
as much as everything else. Especially so now.

The time is now for the full realization to coalesce.

Declarative Music
Phrases such as:
    Low EB $^{\text{A triad}}$ E♭ $^{\text{B triad}}$ E♭ $^{\text{C♯ triad}}$ E♭ $^{\text{B♯ triad}}$ E♭ $^{\text{F triad}}$
    DA $^{\text{DA DAA}}$ DA $^{\text{DA DA DA}}$ DA $^{\text{DA DA DA}}$ D $^{\text{DA DA DA}}$
    And ending by fingering and body pointing (as in opera).
    This can be answered by another instrument.

Lucille:
I want to add some veg. protein to my diet. Some chickpeas. Can
you pick some up? Also herb loose tea.

Fri.
"O.T.Y.O.G."

1. Some improvements seen in this horn's upper parts.
2. Call Broome—rap.
3. "Wrench every note out".
4. Sonny Rollins king of the sax!!
5. I'll meet you at Jim + Andy's. Circa 1956.
6. Call Ronnie Scott.

I could have a new band (modern rock style).

Only tea
Listen tapes
Try to stretch
Send note to guy in Austin
Soak mouth
Pray for help this Sunday
Mon. March 30
No listening—Washington shooting
Too much food eaten
Tues. March 31
No food excess today
So far scrambled egg breakfast

Jerry: Don't forget to always play more up in the beat than below
the beat.
Al: The same holds true. E.g. on "Keep Hold" try to find a way to
keep the accents of the melody thru out the whole tune. There

should be no change in intensity downwards once the blowing section begins. I touched on this before. Also I would like you to solo on "Keep Hold." Around 4s exchanges with me. If you would like to solo on anything else we are doing let me know this too.

Sammy: I would like you to solo on "Island Lady."

Jerry: Watch me on count on oriental welcome. It is 1, 2, 3, 4 AND. The AND is where we are in.

Sonny Rollins Songbook

Introduction

1. 13 to 20 originals with one or two solo choruses included and chords.
2. Notes on each original e.g. when written, who recorded with. Some personal anecdotes.
3. Some photos interspersed throughout.

Tell Lucille there is a big problem of fleas on cats in upstate N.Y.

A hungry cat is a healthy cat.

12lbs—1 can—1/2 can if mixed with dry

7lbs less

Does not recommend fish as diet.

"Never miss a good chance to shut up."
—a wise man on living life.

Sax book to be titled *Horn Culture*

See, I can't make you guys play behind me. I can only ask you to play behind me.

That the propulsion of each number must be present throughout. We want short tight solos. This isn't Music + Art M.S. or Mixells. Each concert had to be tight and precise.

Tommy—*if* you get any drum solos it will be short and precise or else I will have to cut it out of the show. We can trade some 8s and 4s and 2s and whatever by which you are always soloing anyway.

Due to my recent surgery my volume will be reduced considerably, and everything will be much more acoustic level than heretofore.

Man—according to Vedanta philosophy is the greatest being in this universe. And this world is the best in it because only here is the greatest and the best chance for him to become perfect and conquer death.

So the N.A.S.A. has given me an honorary membership! Of course one always likes to be recognized and I am pleased to be so cited. I also want to thank you for whatever part you might have played in making this possible. However, that being said, until there is an attention to the overriding issues now facing PLANET EARTH by such possibly influential organizations as the Alliance we have to feel that a great opportunity is being missed.

Now that I am an honorary member maybe I can find some way to express my feelings to them.

In our world nature is viewed as a source of raw materials and profits.

Christianity has traditionally seen nature as an impersonal stage for the drama of human redemption.

The U.S. has about 50% of the world's wealth but only 6.3% of its population.

When I was a young boy in school we learned all about the French revolution. It was a most inspiring message of how good could triumph over wrong. It forever gave France a place of relevance in my young mind.

Later as I grew up I learned of the Black American soldiers in W.W.I; how they fought valiantly and courageously and we were subsequently honored by France (even as they were shunned by their own country). I learned about James Reese Europe and his extraordinary orchestra (part of that Black American contingent) and also how their music heralded the new age. An age of Democracy and against Fascism. When in the 1920s and '30s Black Jazz musicians and their creation found cultural acceptance in Europe, France led the way. Of course everyone knows of the statue of Sidney Bechet in Juan-les-Pins but does anyone know about the bridge named for Sonny Rollins in France? French musicians and French audiences seem to love me—and I love them.

Music, Physics + Engineering (formerly titled *Musical Engineering*), Harry F. Olson

Otis Spann, *The Blues Never Die*
John Lee Hooker, *That's My Story*
Lonnie Johnson, *Losing Game*

The Sonny Rollins Songbook
(10 Originals with New Solo Choruses)
"Hear What I'm Sayin'"
"Echo-Side Blue"
"Times Slimes"
"And Then My Love I Found You"
"Allison"
"Here's to the People"
"Duke of Iron"
"Wynton"
"Sonnymoon for Two"
"Biji"

Have a nice time in Dusseldorf, so the bellman told me after bringing up my bags. Well—it turned into a tired night for me and besides starting out with an inappropriate opener (not familiar enough to everyone) I just couldn't get my stuff working. I was definitely tired from the travelling and schedule and it is an awful feeling not being able to formulate your ideas on stage. The good thing was that the people were very enthusiastic and loved the band. But the bad news came when on the final number I grabbed the mike to sing the blues. The singing came off pretty good but in grabbing the mike I hit my front tooth with it. It was hit hard but it didn't come out until after the next concert (which I was back to normal for by the way).

"Three Little Words"

Is Jim enough presence when he follows me—should he be as loud?

"Love Letters"

A little low-key after Sonny's opening chorus and into Jim's unaccompanied section.

Sax not that great (for me style-wise)—sax a capella in the style of 1959 again. I don't care for sax here too much—too dated again. If this record states 1959 Sonny clearly maybe O.K.

"Will You Still Be Mine?"

Nice from Sonny's and into Jim's bringing same beginning riff for his solo. Lots of bass drums straight-ahead stuff here. O.K. ending.

"Gone with the Wind"

Rollins's style à la opening melody is still so very much 1959—will this be packaged as "Sonny Rollins + Co" 1959–1961 recording?

Good Jim solo—not crazy about Sonny here but the band is good and swinging under me. Maybe O.K.

"Come Rain Come Shine"

A needed fast tune after G.W.T.W.

Good Jim solos. Sax maybe acceptable. Bass and drums strong together. Maybe usable.

"Sand in My Shoes"

O.K. if you can stand the sax's melody. Very good Jim.

Sax after Jim O.K. if you can stand this playing and intoning. Good ending.

"Brazil"

Good rhythm. Good Jim. Sax sounds too intoning off coming in after Jim's five solo. More Sonny into ending—?

Maybe too long—not enough interest for me—seems too long after sax.

"Alexander's"

What about beginning? Don's entry could be helped by me coming down.

Summum bonum

The supreme good from which all others are derived.

Panjandrums (noun)

Powerful person or pretentious official.

Sophistry

—an argument apparently correct in form. But actually invalid.

Parsimonious—adj.

Frugal to the point of stinginess.

For the past 40 years Sonny Rollins has been making and remaking jazz history, day by day. One of the most inventive improvisors in the history of music. There is the feeling that the truly great artists are gone—Parker, Ellington, Armstrong, Young, Holiday, Tatum, Miles, Coltrane. Rollins is the last remaining Titan, encompassing all of the great stylistic and technical innovations of the post–World War II era.

One day in the future people will be saying, "Yes I once saw Sonny Rollins."

Whiteness is of course a delusion, a scientific and cultural fiction that like all racial identities has no valid formation in biology or anthropology.[4] Whiteness is however a social fact, an identity created and continued with all too real consequences for the distribution of wealth, prestige, and opportunity.

White supremacy is usually less a matter of direct referential and snarling contempt than a system for protecting the privileges of whites by denying communities of color opportunities for asset accumulation and upward mobility.

Certain ideas and thoughts are excluded from our corporate-dominated media, schools, and mainstream political life.

The goal of the ruling interests (corporate) is to keep this society and the entire world open for maximum profitability regardless of the human + environmental costs.

What are we?
Where do we come from?
Where are we going?

Shizen o mamori mashō
Save the environment

It's past time for inhabitants of this planet to face up to what is being done to it. There isn't much time left and any other problem, any other ill, cannot be compared to what we are doing.

We live in a society in which nearly every moment of human attention is exposed to the game plans of spin doctors, image managers, pitchmen, communications consultants, public information officers, and public relations specialists.[5]

Who is enamored of these aspects of our culture, the mind abuse of prime-time television, the dispiriting commercialism, the corporate greed, the ecological desecration, the enduring racialism and denial of same?

Indeed technological advancements coming out of a society of such moral paucity should be a cause of despairing concern to a rational thinking human being. Instead this seems to be of little concern to the T.V.-marinated brains of most people.

Without regard for future generations, corporations treat the environment like a septic tank so long as production costs can be cut, profits maximized, and growth maintained.

The problem with our system is that it best rewards the worst part of us: the ruthless, competitive, conniving, opportunistic, acquisitive drivers giving little rewards and often much punishment or at least handicap to honesty, compassion, fair play, many forms of hard work, love of justice, and a concern for those in need.

It is becoming increasingly apparent that we shall not have the benefits of this world much longer. The imminent and expected destruction of the life cycle of world ecology can only be prevented by a radical shift in outlook from our present naïve conception of this world as a testing ground to a more mature view of the universe as a comprehensive matrix of life forms. Making this shift in viewpoint is essentially spiritual or religious nor economic or political.

In my view the American society has been a curse to mankind and the planet.

The end of economic growth cannot be far off. Economic growth at 3% a conventional standard means the economy doubles every quarter century, typically doubling society's use of raw materials, expenditure of energy, and generation of waste. Obviously this is a system existing as it were on borrowed time. In other words economically we can only hope that other nations never achieve our standard of living. If they did the world would become a desert! Economically America is the bane not the hope of the world. Since the planet is finite as we expand our economy we make it less likely that less developed nations can expand theirs.

Unbridled exploitation of the past and the future in favor of the present.

It is crucial to resist resignation, indifference, the hardening of the heart, and the laziness of the spirit; otherwise one turns into a parasite who is entirely absorbed in the problem of his own metabolism and essentially nothing beyond that interests him.

This government doesn't give a damn about freedom for the people. It has nothing to do with freedom. It's about power, it's about money, it's about racism and elitism and greed. It's about pride and stupidity and ugly insidious forms of paranoia, projection, and delusion but it had nothing to do with a commitment to freedom for the people and even less to do with their well-being.

To make matters worse it appears the majority of the citizens that make up this nation buy into this nationalistic bubble like so many freshly caught carp. Which all serves to remind me of the words of Thomas Jefferson, "I tremble for my country when I reflect that God is just."

Coleman Hawkins, my musical idol, was more than a great tenor saxophonist. At a time when many jazz stars were caught in the trap of alcoholism, drug addiction, and the like, Coleman maintained a dignity befitting of who he was. My own father was a career Navy man who achieved the highest rank possible for those of his background and carried himself with great dignity and pride, just like Coleman did. Hawk was a great role model for us young aspiring musicians who lived in the same neighborhood where we saw him regularly offstage—carrying himself with pride and dignity.

Long live Coleman Hawkins.

I feel tremendously privileged to have succeeded to some extent in a music I continue to believe is the greatest expression of the human spirit.

Freedom Suite and *Way Out West* were concept albums of my invention.

I'm familiar with what needs to be done so I'll try to be as involved as possible.

Yusef Lateef has been a beacon of inspiration to the jazz world and its musicians for many many years. A devout Muslim, Yusef is beloved by Christians, Jews, Buddhists, Hindus, and people of every stripe all over the world. The Gentle Giant has had an enormous spiritual impact on all of us—and always great music.

Films:
Casablanca—Everybody's favorite for the usual reasons but Dooley Wilson's band sealed it for me.

Cabin in the Sky—Duke Ellington, Louis Armstrong, Lena Horne, Ethel Waters . . . You get the idea.

Swing Time—I saw it when I was six and Jerome Kern's music stayed with me.

The Third Man—Austria suffered after the war. Intriguing plot and that great zither music.

A Foreign Affair—Berlin just after the war. A great cast, a great story, and Billy Wilder.

Laura—Who can resist Gene Tierney? The song isn't bad either.

Books:

Hazrat Khan—Sufism—this is what I am musically.

Autobiography of a Yogi—A beautiful story about the soul.

Lies My Teacher Told Me—I love knowledge and education. This is all about re-education.

People's History of the United States—Puts everything in perspective. The story of a nation.

Records:

1. "The Man I Love"—The great Hawk and a masterpiece.
2. "Afternoon of a Basie-ite"—This is Lester Young and all he represents.
3. "Cotton Tail"—The D.E. orchestra in one of its many unforgettable recordings. And of course the mighty Ben Webster up front.
4. "I Can't Get Started"—There's something about this record that gets to me. I can't explain it beyond that.
5. "Unforgettable"—My favorite singer and a good enough song.

6. "Lover Man"—I've been told that is Budd Johnson playing the tenor solo. A great arrangement to cuddle "the Lady."
7. "Billie's Bounce"—Here is the Bird, out of K.C. And listen to the genius of young Miles.
8. "Ballad for Americans"—The great voice—the great man—the great message of this song. And again the great message of this song.
9. "Low Down Dirty Shame"—This is my early youth and the urban instrumental Blues of my main man and his Tympany Five.
10. "I Realize Now"—Nat again—the great trio and I was just learning to slow dance.

Bobby B is one of those extraordinary musicians who can play everything and anything. I love working with him.

Billy Taylor's yeoman's service and devotion to jazz will be hard to replace.

He may be irreplaceable.

I fell in love with Japan the first time I came, many years ago, and I still feel the same thrill and anticipation at the thought of coming again.

In my segment on tenor saxophonists in the recent *Jazz Times* article I neglected to mention the inimitable nonpareil Wayne Shorter. Also I neglected Grover Washington Jr. whose accessible stylings made a big impact.

1. Get sheet music and vocal rendition.
2. Listen carefully to the melody and read the lead sheet carefully then play the song without adding any notes.
3. Get the basic chords (from lead sheet) and memorize them.
4. Arpeggiate the chords in root position.
5. Try to write the melody out from memory.

Madison Square Place is a very interesting place. You can almost feel the spirits there.

My new mantra is "it's all good."

I've deduced an intelligent purpose behind life which (as long as I strive for perfection and am honest with myself) is a positive, nurturing, nourishing immutable essence.

"Technology is the means of going backwards faster."—Huxley[6]

Do you prefer your life to be mechanized and digitalized to the nth degree even if it means using more scarce electricity or would you prefer to sacrifice some personal ease for environmental preservation? Do you need the latest Technogadget to keep ahead of the Joneses or are you willing to step off the consumer treadmill and try to get in touch with more enduring values?

Corporate America, the enthusiastic sponsor of the new technology, knows what it wants: it wants America to buy "stuff." It makes the hard-to-counter, if simplistic, argument that rampant consumerism is the basis of economic growth and prosperity. The Republican party, and many in the Democratic party, knows what it wants as well. These people in the administration and in congress have justified environmental degradation in the name of the "American Way of Life," insisting that wasteful exploitation of energy resources to accommodate more technology is the key to our survival as a people. But to use a somewhat vulgar metaphor... is about to hit the fan as millions of Americans come to grips with what they instinctively feel even if their leaders don't. This will be at the core of politics in these coming years.

H.H. was a true American jazz hero. You know, phenomenally gifted but marginalized by the larger society. I knew Hamp, he was a gentle soul, too pure and fragile for his time but at least some of us witnessed his too short life.

Things have been quite strange here for me even though Lucille had psychologically prepared me for this inevitability. We had been married for almost 50 years after all.

I have recently decided to start back performing (for a while I didn't have any incentive to practice or to contemplate a future!) and that is why I momentarily assumed a resumption of the travel arrangements which were so impeccably handled by Lucille.

Sonny—

   Maybe think about retirement when listening to my playing (technically) at this point.

Got a minute? = jikan aru?

Soon = mō sugu

Someday = itsu-ka

Of course = atarimae-deshō, atarimae-dayo

Maybe = tabun-ne

I'm not sure = yoku-wakaranai

Is that so? = sō-nano?

All right, that's o.k. = daijōbu(dayo)

So am I, me too = watashi-mo or boku-mu

I agree = sansei

It'll be okay, it'll work out = nantoka naru-yo

I'm tired = tsukareteru or tsukareta

I'm sleepy = nemui

So so, not good, not bad = mā mā

What have you been doing? = nani yatteta-no?

I missed you (endearingly) = aitakatta

Okay, I guess = ammari

What's happening? = dō-shita-no?

How's it going? = saikin dō?

I can't say for sure = nanto-mo ienai

This is too good to be true = uso-mitai!!

The great young bassist C. Mc. is an extraordinarily gifted musician who deserves to play with Sonny Rollins again (smiles). He is doing all music and jazz in particular proud. All hail.

The honorable and venerable Jim Hall is here with me tonite commemorating our successful collaborations of years past. Jim is the class of his instrument. His playing never fails to inspire me.

There is a hallowed legacy that passes down from Louis Armstrong and such. It must be earned but has to be bestowed from above as it were.

It has come to my attention that the great jazz musician and my former colleague Johnny Griffin has agreed to have his legacy archived at the university. I think this is an excellent development and further indicates Duke's dedication to the highest standards in all aspects of education.

I'm very proud to have received an honorary doctorate from D.U. some years ago.

It was always an honor to appear with one of my musical heroes, Miles Davis.

When Branford Marsalis appeared on the scene what seems like just a few years ago he brought with him the technical proficiency and creative gifts of the new jazz musician. The world of music and the world of jazz in particular are lucky to have him.

Greetings *Jazz Japan* readers,

Congratulations on your new magazine. But I have a question for you and for every person in Japan as well. What is jazz?

This is my answer.

Jazz is life as shown thru music.

Jazz is life in musical form.

Jazz is the musical expression of life.

As we know life changes every second. Each snowflake that falls is different. Every sunrise is different. Every sunset is different. The clouds in the sky are never the same—always changing. Jazz mimics life. Real jazz music is changing from note to note. When I play my horn I can never play the same note in the same way twice. Just like life. Every moment is a new beginning. Even if I'm playing the same song it's different each time I play it. That's why they call jazz the music of surprise, the greatest and most challenging music in the world. If it's good jazz it's fresh, it's new, it's exciting. It's the music of the heavens. It's called jazz.

Dear Michelle Obama,

Thank you so much for the hospitality and kindness with which you received us at the recent Gala and earlier this year at the medal awards. I told Barack at the medal awards that I was originally for Kucinich but that I'm now with him. I hope he forgave me.

I'm writing today to draw your attention to the N.E.A.'s cancelling of the Jazz Masters program. I remember you telling me about your father and grandfather's love and appreciation for jazz music and I was so touched. The strength, beauty and moral spirituality of this music has meant so much for generations of striving black Americans. That it has kindled the spirit of freedom in every corner of the globe says so much about its universality and what America really stands for and represents for human beings everywhere.

I know this is cost cutting time but the Jazz Masters program gives back so much more than it costs. The men of genius who are largely unheralded (unlike myself) represent irreplaceable beacons whose light is spread forward to generations and backwards to generations. For jazz music is not a fad. It has no beginning and it has no endings. I'm sure there are other expenditures which are important. But this is another important one.

Once again thanks for the genuine warmth we felt coming from you both at the White House. And what about 4 more years!!

Which is best, interpretation or song? In any case, jazz and standards are forever locked in loving embrace.

You can't live on money.

Bhakti—the path of love as it were.
Jnana—the path of knowledge.
Karma—dedicating all fruits of one's action to the divine source.

One works not for one's self but for the glory of a higher union in gratitude to a greater good as it were.

Dear President Clinton,

It was great finally meeting you at the State Dept. dinner. I have been a supporter of yours from when you first emerged on the scene as Gov. of Arkansas. I also want to thank you for the kind and laudatory remarks you made about my career. Many people including myself wished they had been made part of the following night's T.V. presentation.

All in all though it was quite an affair and the American people were given a glimpse of this American music which as you know they are so rarely exposed to. It was in this sense that it occurred to me that the moment not be wasted.

Gifted but economically disadvantaged youngsters (from all strata of the American landscape by the way) should be made eligible for tuition scholarships. To help make this happen I want to start the Sonny Foundation or the Sonny Rollins Foundation. By the way I have learned to be a humble person and am not interested in the perpetuation of my name in the establishment of such a foundation but have been advised that it is necessary to have it named so. So, so be it.

The objective is giving young gifted people a chance to make something of their lives for themselves, their country and the world community.

As you probably know the establishment of such foundations requires a board of directors. I would like to have you sit on the board. In fact I would be honored to have you do so. I am currently searching for the other board members and am preparing mission statements and so on. I have in fact already been pledged a contribution from a well-known foundation and have been told that other contributions should be no problem in acquiring once it is set up.

Again, it is about making a difference in a quite negative world. I do hope you will consider it.

Best wishes

I was so fortunate to be born in Harlem and to be exposed to so much great music. Fats Waller in particular made me realize early on that there was nothing in the world greater than jazz. Then Louis Jordan made me want to play the saxophone. My dear mom got me a second-hand alto sax and I was on my way. However it was around age nine that I heard the record of Coleman Hawkins's "Body and Soul" blaring out from juke boxes all over the place that my life's journey was laid open for me. Improvisation without words, just that sax speaking, talking to everyone. Musical Mastery. Strong intellectual as well as visceral emotion—this was and still is the epitome of the great musical solo statement.

What Coleman did was amazing in that he improvised an instrumental piece of such complexity that it is still being studied today, and which completely engaged the masses.

Enjoyment is the million-headed monster that we must tread underfoot.[7]

The world is a demon. It is a kingdom of which the puny ego is king. Put it away and stand firm. Give up lust and gold and fame

149

and hold fast to the Lord and at last we shall reach a state of perfect indifference. The idea that the gratification of the senses constitutes enjoyment is purely materialistic. There is not one spark of real enjoyment there; all the joy there is, is a mere reflection of the true bliss.

Live in the body—but not of it.

Neither seek nor avoid; take what comes. It is liberty to be affected by nothing; do not merely endure, be unattached.

With animals and with the lowest human beings who are very much like animals happiness is all in the body.

Forgive everyone everything.

What other people think of you is none of your business.

No matter how you feel, get up, dress up, and show up.

Notes

1. The phrase "so mote it be" is used as part of Masonic and Rosicrucian rituals; Rollins had a longstanding interest in Rosicrucianism, and his archives include a copy of *Uncommon Men*, a pamphlet published by the Supreme Grand Lodge of the Ancient Mystical Order Rosae Crucis in 1960. Rollins sketched his own face over the concluding paragraphs, opposite a biography of Michael Faraday.
2. Rollins was greatly influenced by the circular breathing techniques of pioneering bebop saxophonist Kermit "Scotty" Scott, which he referred to as "Scotty breathing" in his mentor's honor.
3. Rollins takes this phrase from Robert Schumann, as quoted in Kurt Pahlen's *Music of the World: A History*, trans. James A. Galston (New York: Crown, 1949).
4. Here Rollins is quoting from George Lipsitz, *The Possessive Investment in Whiteness: How White People Profit from Identity Politics* (Philadelphia: Temple University Press, 1998), vii–viii.
5. In this section, Rollins opens by paraphrasing the historian Stuart Ewen's *PR!: A Social History of Spin* (New York: Basic Books, 1996), 19. His fifth paragraph adapts the leftist scholar Michael Parenti, who writes, "The problem with capitalism is that it best rewards the worst part of us: ruthless, competitive, conniving, opportunistic, acquisitive drives, giving little reward and often much punishment—or at least much handicap—to honesty, compassion, fair play, many forms of hard work, love of justice, and a concern for those in need" (*Land of Idols: Political Mythology in America* [New York: St. Martin's Press, 1994], 84).
6. Rollins condenses Huxley's original phrasing: "Technological progress has merely provided us with more efficient means of going backwards."
7. Here Rollins quotes two passages from Swami Vivekananda's *Inspired Talks* (The Ramakrishna Mission, 1910), 78, 74. The annotations—"Live in the body—but not of it" and "With animals and with the lowest human beings who are very much like animals happiness is all in the body"—are Rollins's own synthesis of Vivekananda's thoughts.

SONNY ROLLINS (b. 1930) has been called "jazz's greatest living improviser" by *The New York Times*. Born in New York City and raised in its Harlem neighborhood, Rollins began his career playing alto saxophone but soon switched to the instrument that he would become renowned for, the tenor sax. He has recorded with musicians such as Miles Davis, Charlie Parker, and Thelonious Monk; composed a number of jazz standards; and been honored with the Grammy Lifetime Achievement Award and a National Medal of Arts, among other awards.

SAM V. H. REESE is a critic and short-story writer. His most recent book is *Blue Notes: Jazz, Literature, and Loneliness*. Originally from New Zealand, he lives and teaches in the United Kingdom.